RAISING A **MODERN-DAY**

JOSEPH

A TIMELESS STRATEGY FOR GROWING GREAT KIDS

RAISING A MODERN-DAY JOSEPH

JOSEPH

A TIMELESS STRATEGY FOR GROWING GREAT KIDS

LARRY FOWLER

David C Cook®

transforming lives together

RAISING A MODERN-DAY JOSEPH
Published by David C. Cook
4050 Lee Vance View
Colorado Springs, CO 80918 U.S.A.
David C. Cook Distribution Canada
55 Woodslee Avenue, Paris, Ontario, Canada N3L 3E5

David C. Cook U.K., Kingsway Communications
Eastbourne, East Sussex BN23 6NT, England

David C. Cook and the graphic circle C logo
are registered trademarks of Cook Communications Ministries.

The Web site addresses recommended throughout this book are offered as a resource
to you. These Web sites are not intended in any way to be or imply an endorsement
on the part of David C. Cook, nor do we vouch for their content.

All Scripture quotations are taken from the *Holy Bible, New International Version*®. *NIV*®.
Copyright © 1973, 1978, 1984 by International Bible Society. Used by permission of
Zondervan. All rights reserved. All italics in Scripture are added by the author for emphasis.

LCCN 2008935941
ISBN 978-1-4347-6705-9

© 2009 Awana® Clubs International

The Team: Don Pape, Thomas Womack, Amy Kiechlin, Jack Campbell, and Karen Athen
Cover Design: Amy Kiechlin

Printed in the United States of America
First Edition 2009

1 2 3 4 5 6 7 8 9 10

082808

To my parents, Margaret and Mervin Fowler, who consistently modeled the godly lifestyle and behaviors seen in the Old Testament Joseph. I am deeply indebted to you, as are my children, grandchildren, and the generations to follow them, for the legacy of godliness that you have established.

CONTENTS

INTRODUCTION

KNOW, LOVE, SERVE

I am passionate about discipling children to *know, love,* and *serve* Jesus Christ.

I've become so enamored with those three words. They form a triumvirate that rules over my direction, my choices, and my actions as a father, a grandfather, a children's ministry worker in my church, and a children's ministry executive.

I wish I could say that grouping of words was original with me, but Christian leaders have no doubt used them together down through the centuries. My organization, Awana, has adopted the phrase in our Hope and Prayer Statement: "that all children and youth will come to know, love, and serve the Lord Jesus Christ." Since we've adopted the statement, those three words have increasingly driven me, focused me, and motivated me. Here's how:

First, they keep me *balanced.* I haven't always been so balanced in how I disciple children. Sometimes I've overemphasized the "know" component in my ministry, to the neglect of the "love" component. For many years, I haven't thought much at all about building in the "serve." Now, I try to think regularly about all three.

- *Knowing* means children's heads are involved. But that's not enough.

- *Loving* means children's hearts are involved. But that's not enough either.
- *Serving* means children's hands are involved. This, too, is insufficient by itself.

If I, as a growing disciple of Christ, have only two of these elements in combination, my growth is lacking. Think about it. Without *knowing*, I'm misguided, even if I love and serve. Without *loving*, I'm empty, even if I serve and know. And without *serving*, I'm disobedient, even if I know and love.

Beyond keeping me balanced, *know, love,* and *serve* provide insight into sequence, helping us keep the cart behind the horse. Here's what I mean:

To serve rightly, I must love the One I serve.

To love rightly, I must know the One I love.

To know more fully, I will serve the One I know.

Knowing is never the end; neither is loving. In fact, there *is* no end: The more I know Christ, the more I'll love Him; the more I love Him, the more I'll serve Him; the more I serve Him, the more I'll know Him.

But there *is* a beginning: It's really hard to love someone you don't know, and so "know" comes first. Of course, in regard to Jesus Christ, *know* is full of implications. It certainly includes "knowing about" Jesus Christ, but so much more.

First, it means that one knows Him as his or her Savior. Trusting in the work of Jesus Christ on the cross to pay the penalty for our sins and in His resurrection from the dead to provide power for living changes us radically. We go from having no relationship with

Him at all to not only having such a relationship, but having Him live within us!

Since no one truly knows Jesus Christ without a relationship and the relationship comes through faith in the gospel, evangelism comes first in priority. We *must* share the gospel with our children and young people as our primary mission.

Second, *knowing* includes an experiential aspect. Obedience and fellowship with Jesus Christ produce a deeper, more satisfying level of knowledge. The apostle John states it this way:

> We know that we have come to know him if we obey his commands. The man who says, "I know him," but does not do what he commands is a liar, and the truth is not in him. (1 John 2:3–4)

Yet, *how?* How do we help children to know, love, and serve Jesus Christ? How do parents do it? How do churches? How do children's ministries and youth ministries? *Are* we doing it? Are we doing it *well?* These are questions I'll address in this book.

Want to test how effective we are? How about: Take a typical seventeen-year-old from your church, and plant him right in the middle of a godless, pagan, hedonistic culture. Separate him from his family. Strip him of his spiritual support system. Fire several dozen rounds of alluring temptations at him. Treat him unfairly again and again. Then feed his ego with promotions and success. How confident are you that your seventeen-year-old would continually demonstrate that he knows, loves, and serves God through all that?

That was exactly the test given to the Old Testament Joseph. You know the result: He passed with flying colors. This fascinating young man knew God, loved God, and served Him well throughout his whole time in Egypt.

This book includes a look at Joseph, and we'll also look at today's young people and how we can disciple them to be Josephs in a culture that's too much like the Egypt of Joseph's day.

And don't be surprised if you, too, become more enamored than ever with those three words: *know, love,* and *serve.*

CHAPTER 1

THE MOST DIFFICULT MOMENT IN PARENTING

What would you say is the most difficult moment of parenting?

Parenting in a real sense is the process of letting go. When our little baby comes home from the hospital, we start with complete control of that baby's life; but we also begin letting go. First, it's letting them sit up without support. In a few months, it's letting them walk around the coffee table. It's like we have this tight, controlling grip at the beginning, and then we gradually start letting go, one finger at a time. For most parents, loosening each finger is difficult.

Sending a child to kindergarten is a difficult moment. You're controlling with only nine fingers now, or maybe eight. Years later, another big challenge is allowing your child to drive alone for the first time at age sixteen or seventeen. By then your grip is down to three or four fingers, if that.

But when you completely open that last finger, finally releasing your child entirely to his own decisions, his own common sense, his own wisdom—that's the toughest. It's what I call the MDM, the Most Difficult Moment:

For most parents, the most difficult moment
is when you come face-to-face with the reality
that you've given up all control.

That moment may come while driving away from the dorm parking lot of a son or daughter's college. Or the moment of lingering as the military bus disappears into the distance. Or driving home after a daughter's wedding. Or the last trip carrying a son's possessions from his room to his car on the day he moves out.

We usually know it's coming. Our teenage child plans for college, applies, anticipates, and packs. But planning and preparation don't help when that actual moment comes; they don't take away the monstrous lump in our throat that nearly chokes us as we realize the one we worked hard to raise is now on his own. Dad thinks, "What will he do? Will he make wise choices? Who will he pick for friends?" Mom worries, "Will he know where to get help if he gets sick?" They both wonder, "Will he party? Will he do drugs?" Christian parents worry, "Will he follow God? Will he choose Christian friends? Will he go to church?"

My good friend and coworker Dave Pearson has had a passion for ministry to children and youth his whole life. While he ministers effectively as a leader and speaker, his first concern is for his own children. He relates his own MDM as he experienced it on a plane ride from Phoenix to Chicago, after getting his eighteen-year-old daughter settled in for her first year of college in Arizona, two thousand miles from home.

As I got on the plane, it felt like I was losing my little girl. Would she ever come home? Will she be able to make it on her own? Will she follow the Lord in what she does? Will I ever see her again? Now, I knew in my head God had made some promises, but I wasn't feeling them in my heart. Is God as faithful as He says He is? Would He make good on His promises? Would His protection be enough without my help? I was forced to put my money where my mouth has been most of my life. I'd never before had my faith stretched like this; this was *my little girl* we were talking about! It was the most difficult plane trip of my life.

My own MDM also had to do with leaving a child at college. Ryan, our youngest, wanted to attend college in Southern California where he grew up, though we'd moved to Illinois. For financial reasons, he decided to attend a junior college near Simi Valley, where he'd graduated from high school.

With a junior college, there's no orientation, no welcome, and no dorms. You just register and attend. Unlike local residents going to school there, Ryan had to find a room to rent for the year.

I flew to Los Angeles and spent the morning with him as he registered, then we got out the want ads and began looking for a place for him to live. After driving past several hole-in-the-wall places, we found a room in a house that was clean and in a good neighborhood. The owner and his son lived there too, so it felt like an okay environment for Ryan. The medieval decor bothered me some; what kind of person would put knight's armor in the entry to their living room?

But it was the best we found, so we signed the rental contract and moved him in.

As I was leaving Ryan in a pretty strange house, I could tell he was nervous about being completely on his own. He would now be completely determining his own schedule, his own friends, his own life patterns, his own values. I knew he could take care of himself, but I couldn't stop the nagging sense that I was abandoning him. I knew God was still in control, but I wrestled with the reality that I wasn't.

As I got in the car and drove to the airport that night, I couldn't stop the tears for most of the way. In some ways, it was like dealing with a death; there was the grief over *my* loss: I no longer had Ryan home. There was also the finality of it. My role as a parent was permanently changed. I knew I was only an influencer now—no longer in control—and my influence would be only from a distance. There was also the uncertainty of the future. What kind of decisions would Ryan make? Would he stay safe? Would he follow God? Like my friend Dave in his MDM, I struggled with practicing my faith. It was difficult giving up control (not that I had a lot, but you know what I mean).

Ryan survived that semester, and so did I. Today he's a fantastic young man, with whom I'm greatly pleased—and I know God is too.

THE FATHER OF JOSEPH

Two contrasting Bible stories graphically illustrate this MDM of parenting. Both stories are about sons leaving home, out from under their parents' control; and they focus on two dads who must have deeply grieved on their day of losing control.

First, there's the Old Testament Jacob. Undoubtedly his MDM as a parent comes as he hears evidence from his other sons that their brother Joseph had been killed. (It would be many long years of separation before Jacob found out otherwise.) Understandably, Jacob was deeply grieved:

> Then Jacob tore his clothes, put on sackcloth and mourned for his son many days. All his sons and daughters came to comfort him, but he refused to be comforted. "No," he said, "in mourning will I go down to the grave to my son." So his father wept for him. (Gen. 37:34–35)

A large number of parents will identify a tragic event like the death of a child as their MDM. That was the case with our dear friends Bob and Lee Baldwin, with whom we worked closely in ministry years ago.

At their church in Southern California, Bob served on Sunday mornings as the sound technician, and part of his duties was to close and lock up the church. One Easter Sunday, Bob stayed behind after the service to help lock up while Lee and their three boys went on ahead to her father's house for an Easter meal with a large number of their extended family.

Bob arrived late, just as after-dinner preparations were underway for a big Easter egg hunt, a highlight of the afternoon. The adults went to the front yard to hide eggs after leaving the numerous kids inside the house. Meanwhile Bob fixed himself a plate of food and headed out back along with a friend. The two men sat on the patio near a swimming pool.

What no one noticed was that Bob and Lee's three-year-old, Chad, had stayed in the backyard and was playing with a toy car by the edge of the pool. Bob and his friend never saw him. The car fell into the pool; trying to retrieve it, little Chad went into the water as well. He slipped beneath the pool cover and couldn't find his way out.

After about ten minutes, the adults came in from the front yard, realized Chad was missing, and started the frantic search. By the time they finally found him, it was too late. Bob and Lee lost their precious little boy in a horrible accident.

I'm sure you can imagine Bob's feelings that day as he realized his son had died so near to where he was sitting. Bob had to live with the grieving, but also with the "if onlys" that haunted him: "If only I'd looked over at the pool"; "If only I'd counted the kids"; "If only I'd been faster about locking up the church and getting here."

Some parents have other experiences that are deeply tragic. It might be the moment of learning about a case of abuse, or about cancer, or about some other devastation.

Fortunately, not all parents must go through such tragic moments. But even though their MDMs lack the terrible permanence of something like the death of a child, their experiences still involve emotional intensity, separation, and grief. And they all share this aspect in common: loss of control.

THE FATHER OF THE PRODIGAL

In the New Testament, I think the father in the story of the prodigal son would also have picked his younger son's parting as his MDM of parenting. The father isn't named (characteristic of Jesus' parables) and may not even be real; but in his actions toward his wayward son, he certainly represents our heavenly Father's love, forgiveness, and grace toward us. That was Jesus' point.

But I want you to see another perspective. Look again at the first few lines of the parable:

> There was a man who had two sons. The younger one said to his father, "Father, give me my share of the estate." So he divided his property between them.
>
> Not long after that, the younger son got together all he had, set off for a distant country. (Luke 15:11–13)

Can you imagine what the father was feeling as he watched this son—who had made such an unwise request—ride off with more money than he was responsible enough to handle? *What's this immature kid thinking? What's going to happen to him?* Imagine the knot in his stomach and the lump in his throat as his son shrank into a tiny dot on the horizon.

No doubt the father of the Prodigal had lots of uncertainty as he watched his son leave. We, too, often experience such uncertainty as we wonder how our kids will respond to independence.

JOSEPH OR THE PRODIGAL?

When parents begin to see signs that their children are struggling spiritually, they often direct their angst toward the church: "Help us raise our kids!" they beg. Many times the children's and youth ministries at our churches do help; too often, the help isn't enough.

That's where the story of Joseph and the contrasting parable of the prodigal son become so applicable today. No parent ever wants their son or daughter to respond to independence like the Prodigal. But in reality, our MDMs are often made more difficult because we fear our child will make bad choices like he did.

Likewise, no congregation desires their youth to walk away from church once they leave for college. Yet few churches really have a thorough understanding of what happens to those children who grew up in their ministries.

Every Christian parent, I believe, wants their son or daughter to be like Joseph, and every church shares that desire with them. Our MDMs become far less traumatic if we can have confidence that our children will make wise decisions and choices when they're away from our control.

Regretfully, far too many Christian young people who leave home act like the Prodigal; too few live like Joseph. In this book, you'll discover the critical need for a new course, examine Joseph as a model for churches and parents to target, and learn of a path that will better produce the young adults we want to see.

My prayer is that God will open your eyes to new approaches to guiding children spiritually as you read this book.

DISCUSSION GUIDE

1. At this point in your parenting experience, can you think of a difficult moment when you've had to let go of control?

2. What do you think of the proposal that, generally speaking, the Most Difficult Moment is when you release control entirely?

3. Do you remember when you stepped completely out from under your parents' control? What do you think this was like for them?

4. Why is it helpful for you as a parent to think ahead to the MDM and consider what it might be like?

5. What do you think it would have been like to be the father of the Prodigal? Do you know of any parallel situations today?

6. What would it have been like to be Jacob and hear of his son's death? How would you have expected it to affect him? Do you know of any evidence in the story later on to indicate that he *was* still affected?

CHAPTER 2

THE CHRISTIAN KID NEXT DOOR

Sarah[1] was the daughter of our next-door neighbors, and every week she went with them to the same church we attended. We watched her grow up, and we were certain she would always be her parents' pride and joy. At church she was the brightest student, always eager to please her Sunday school teachers. Sarah knew answers to Bible questions before the other kids did, and she was well-behaved. She participated in the kids' puppet ministry. She seemed to have all the makings of a future godly woman.

Today, Sarah is in her third year of college, openly sleeping with her boyfriend and boozing it up on a regular basis. She goes to church only when home with her parents (after they beg and plead). Sarah still claims to be saved, and her conversation demonstrates that she knows "Christianese." Yet little in her life reflects the Christian influences in her upbringing. She hasn't forgotten Bible facts, but rarely bases her decisions on them. She seems happy with the knowledge that she once "accepted Jesus as her Savior" (her "hell insurance?"), but cares nothing about living a Christian life.

We and others at our church who have known Sarah question privately what went wrong. Were her parents too lenient? Too strict? Maybe two-faced? Didn't they really practice their Christian walk in the home? We figured they must have done *something* wrong, even if we didn't know what.

How many Christian kids like Sarah do you know? Too often we watch the kids of other families grow into young adults and shake our heads at how they're turning out.

But if we're transparent, we have to admit (though it's embarrassing to do so) that the Christian kid in our own house is also a spiritual disappointment. Yes, our own son or daughter isn't doing so well in following God. We watch them care far more about text messages from friends than the Bible text. When they hear "message," they think first of their cell phone, not the youth pastor's words. They amaze us with how fast they navigate online, yet how slow they are in finding things in the Bible.

As Christian parents, we're in an uncomfortable position. Deeply concerned, we're hoping *our* neighbors aren't noticing *our* kid like we noticed Sarah.

IS THE CRISIS REAL?

Christians had better wake up.

We're losing our kids—fast!

Or are we? More and more attention has been given to this reality in the last decade—but some don't really believe it's anything new or significant. After all, they say, kids have always had to work through the struggle to adopt the faith of their parents as their own. Teenagers have always rebelled, and always wrestled with the temptations of the world. It's just in the nature of that life stage. Right?

What's the truth? Do we have a major problem that's getting worse? Or are the researchers just trying to sell books?

Nearly every report of research on the spirituality of Christian teenagers or young adults in America is, at best, bleak. Many are almost doomsday-like in their assessment.

Christian leaders point to Western Europe and say, "We're right behind them on the slippery slope." From personal observation, I agree Europe is on a downward spiral. I saw it firsthand in Denmark. I was the keynote speaker recently at a national children's workers conference. My key contact was Marianne, the children's pastor from Denmark's largest church. Marianne is deeply committed to children's ministry, passionate about being a follower of Christ, and burdened for her country. In addition, she has a remarkable personal heritage in children's work—most notably, her father was the children's pastor in the same church a generation earlier. But Marianne's challenge is so much greater. While she had two hundred children in her program (yes, the largest in Denmark), her father had overseen a ministry in the same church up to two *thousand* children.

Such a decline is representative of churches throughout their country. I got the impression from other ministry leaders that fifteen to twenty children is considered a large group for a church. Most of the children's workers were tired, discouraged, and in desperate need of hope for the future.

Denmark, a country that once sent out thousands of missionaries and had a huge impact on the world, has slipped in a little over

one generation from being a main player in Christianity to being a
bit player.

Are we watching it happen in America right now?

If so, are we too far gone?

WHAT RESEARCH SAYS

The conclusions of research about how our Christian kids are turning out are not unanimous, but the vast majority of the findings say
our young adults are in a lot of trouble spiritually.

Many people in our American churches, however, are either
ignoring the research or dismissing it.

One online reviewer for my previous book, *Rock-Solid Kids*,
praised it by saying, "It's not just alarmist statistics." I was at first
quite pleased and appreciated her comment. Then I thought about
her choice of words. *Alarmist?* Is that how she views the statistics
about our children and youth? Why did she say alarm*ist* rather than
alarm*ing?* Doesn't she believe the research? Is she that tired of hearing
doom-and-gloom reports?

Her comment begs critical questions: *Is* the research alarmist?
Are those who are speaking out crying wolf? Is all this only a cultural twist that's being painted as a crisis? Or is the crisis real? Is it
something with the potential to obliterate the vitality and future of
Christianity in America?

Consider what's being said:

DECLINING COMMITMENT

As Christian young people leave home for college and work,
they're leaving the church and the faith of their parents.

Christian researcher George Barna reports that one of every two teenagers abandons the church during college. "In fact," he says, "the most potent data regarding disengagement is that a majority of twentysomethings—61 percent of today's young adults—had been churched at one point during their teen years but they are now spiritually disengaged."[2]

Meanwhile Josh McDowell says that some denominational leaders report that as many as 94 percent of teenagers leave the church after high school.[3]

LifeWay Publications reported this finding: "More than two-thirds of young adults who attend a Protestant church for at least a year in high school will stop attending church regularly for at least a year between the ages of 18 and 22." Their research found that some of these eventually returned: Among 23-to-30-year-olds who had previously stopped attending church, thirty-five percent were now attending at least twice a month. Nevertheless, the LifeWay report reached this conclusion:

> There is no easy way to say it, but it must be said. Parents and churches are not passing on a robust Christian faith and an accompanying commitment to the church. We can take some solace in the fact that many do eventually return. But, Christian parents and churches need to ask the hard question, "What is it about our faith commitment that does not find root in the lives of our children?"[4]

UNBIBLICAL WORLDVIEWS

Christian young people are not transferring the biblical knowledge they have into a biblical worldview. McDowell estimates only

15 percent of Christian young people have a biblical worldview. Barna says it's less than 10 percent.[5]

Has it always been this way, or is this a new phenomenon? After all, *worldview* became a popular buzzword only in recent decades.

Moreover, worldview can be nearly impossible to measure. We can track trends and make general statements, but that's about all. The true measure of worldview is not found in answers to a survey or multiple-choice test, but in the real decisions of life. Will the seventeen-year-old newly behind the wheel respond with Christlikeness when another driver cuts him off? What about the new college student who for the first time in her life has the freedom to determine where she sleeps? Will she say no to her boyfriend who wants her beside him? At boot camp, will the Marine recruit witness to his buddies, like he was told and trained to do in his church's youth group? Those are the real tests of worldview.

DECLINING BIBLE KNOWLEDGE

Christian young people don't know nearly as much about the Bible as they used to.

Christian Smith, principal investigator of the National Study of Youth and Religion, concludes that "adolescent religious and spiritual understanding and concern seem to be generally very weak. Most U.S. teens have a difficult to impossible time explaining what they believe, what it means, and what the implications of their beliefs are for their lives."[6] While that was likely true in previous generations as well, is it even more prevalent today?

I asked Pat Blewett, Dean of the College at Columbia International University, how he viewed the Bible knowledge of incoming college freshmen. He said that ten to fifteen years ago, the average score for freshmen on the college's Bible knowledge test was about 60 percent; now it's less than 40 percent.

Perhaps the greater tragedy is the number of Christian colleges and universities who are no longer concerned enough about biblical knowledge even to test students on it. Instead, many now test for spiritual formation without any concern for the biblical foundation on which true maturity comes.

In late 2005, Awana asked two questions of a hundred Bible colleges and seminaries: (1) "Do you measure the Bible knowledge of incoming freshmen?" (2) "If so, have you seen a trend in their scores over the past ten years?" Fifty-eight schools responded. A number of responses included comments such as these:

> The general consensus of the Bible and theology faculty is that there has been a marked decrease in the level of Bible knowledge in recent years. It seems that even students who have gone to church all their lives are not as biblically literate as students in years gone by. (David Reese, Toccoa Falls College)

> I have been teaching at Puget Sound Christian College for 23 years in the Bible department. The level of Bible knowledge for incoming students has decreased dramatically over this period. Our assumption now is that incoming freshmen know nothing about the Bible, and that we must start at the most basic level. (Mark S. Krause, Dean, Puget Sound Christian College)

Fifteen years ago, there definitely was a "center" group in our Intro to Bible classes, comprising the majority of students in each class who shared a similar level of knowledge coming in to Bethel. But in recent years, we have lost the "center" of our Intro to Bible courses. Students arrive on campus either knowing very little or a great deal. There is no longer a "center" to teach to, so we plan to begin testing, so we can group students by incoming knowledge. (Dr. Michael W. Holmes, Chair, Biblical and Theological Studies Department, Bethel University)

Gary Burge, professor of New Testament at Wheaton College, reports the following surprising results from Wheaton's monitoring of biblical literacy among incoming freshmen (who represent almost every Protestant denomination):

- One-third couldn't put the following in order: Abraham, the Old Testament prophets, the death of Christ, and Pentecost.
- Half couldn't sequence the following: Isaac's birth, Moses in Egypt, Saul's death, and Judah's exile.
- One-third could not identify Matthew as an apostle from a list of New Testament names.
- Half did not know that the Christmas story can be found in Matthew; one-third didn't know that Paul's travels are recorded in Acts; half didn't know that the Passover story is in Exodus.

Burge's conclusion is that biblical illiteracy is at a crisis level not just in our culture but throughout America's churches.[7]

Not all the research is gloom-and-doom. Researchers at the University of Texas at Austin found in their study that only 20 percent of students said there was a decline in the importance of religion, and only 17 percent had disaffiliated from their religion. (The study was done across all religions, not just evangelical Christianity.) This would seem to paint a different picture than the other reports I've cited.

However, in the same study, 69 percent reported a decline in their church attendance. The declines were especially evident in students who chose to smoke marijuana, live together, or participate in drinking binges. For evangelical Protestants, 63 percent reported a decline in their attendance; the rate was even higher—three-fourths—among mainline Protestants and Catholics.[8]

That tells us there's a big gap. Many young adults *say* faith is important to them, but their practice reveals something different. Sarah, the next-door girl I mentioned earlier, would be part of that majority who say their faith is still important to them, while in practice she has completely abandoned the pursuit of godliness.

RETHINKING

If this research doesn't cause parents and churches to self-inspect, I don't know what will. It has certainly done that for me. It's made me rethink how I raised my own children (with too many regrets), focus more on how I spend my time with my grandchildren, and be far more diligent in my ministry with children in my church.

While some of the research methods, questions, and conclusions may be suspect, I'm completely persuaded that George Barna was right in 2002 when he said, "We have virtually lost a generation of young people; we dare not lose another."

There *is* a crisis. There *is* a decline. I can see it in the kids I work with today. I see it in the children who attend Awana Clubs. I see it in many of the parents I know. So many of them don't fully realize that as our Christian young people leave the nest, their life choices are influenced by all their developmental years, especially by the nature of the foundation they received up to age twelve. That's a critical window of opportunity for both worldview development and for a child to respond to the gospel and place his or her faith in Christ.

THE POSITIVE SIDE

You would think the results of the research would cause people to spring into action, revitalizing children's ministry, informing parents, and throwing new energy at the need. And to some extent, that has happened. There has been some progress.

In the past decade, the cry for awareness about the state of our Christian youth has increased.

- A significant number of parents are deeply devoted to the spiritual discipleship of their children. *You,* in fact, may be doing great with your children. You and your church may be focused on this issue, and you're doing something about it. Praise God for you! Keep it up.
- More books about children and youth ministry are being written, and they're being read not just by ministry specialists but by many other concerned adults as well.
- Children's ministry and family ministry are receiving greater attention. New ministries have sprung up, and several that have

been around for a while are flourishing. Many are giving particular attention to the need for greater parent involvement.

• Many churches are adding the position of family pastor, or some version of it, to give emphasis to this part of ministry.

• Christian colleges and universities are taking notice. In 2003, I could count only two with a children's ministry major; now the number is over fifty. Still others are adding a family ministries major. Many believe this is mirroring the phenomenon of the 1970s, when youth ministry received ever-increasing attention until nearly every Christian college of any size established a youth ministries major.

IS THERE PROGRESS?

But is all this enough?

Here are three critical questions:

1. Are parents now taking responsibility for the spiritual upbringing of their children?

2. Is there improvement in our young adults' commitment to Christ once they leave home?

3. Are we seeing a trend in our young adults toward a deeper, more biblical worldview?

In 2003, George Barna's book *Transforming Children into Spiritual Champions* had a huge impact, bolstering the priority of children's ministry and creating conversations and actions around what we can do better. Since then, despite years of increasing attention on the importance of children's ministry and on the priority of parent involvement, I see little change in the dozens of churches I have contact with. There's little change in children's ministry and little change in the approach to parents. It's too early to tell if there's a change in our youth, but I'm not convinced we've done enough.

That's not to say there's *no* change. Many thousands of parents, I believe, have become serious and more focused on raising their own children to be devoted followers of Christ—but it needs to be millions. Many hundreds of churches are quite aware of the crisis and are doing what they can to address it—but thousands more need to join them.

The chart to the right shows what I think has happened in the past ten years in regard to the awareness factor. The world of children's ministry has enjoyed much greater attention. But is it enough? Will we continue to improve, or 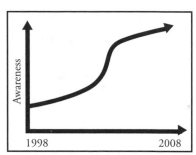 was it a minifad that will see the downward side of a bell curve?

Where will the arrow be in five years? ten years?

Several churches have provided leadership in change, and for that they're to be commended. But the vast majority of our Christian families and our young people are in churches that *haven't* changed, and those churches—and the families in them—must also refocus and address the problem if the church in America is to change.

I may be oversimplifying the situation to some degree, but here's where I think we are:

- In the small church, in which children's and youth ministry are led by a volunteer, one rarely finds a purposeful ministry design, an overall direction, or deliberate connections with parents.

- Large churches nearly always *appear* to have their act together, but underneath the surface many programs are only loosely connected, and they're needs-based rather than connected to a long-term discipleship objective. For many, there's also the pressure for "numbers growth" over substance. A significant number of children's pastors in large churches have told me they feel constant pressure to produce bigger numbers or else their jobs are at risk.

- Ethnic church leaders are concerned with a strong worship focus. That's good, but this emphasis is often so strong that it results in little attention left for children's ministry, which is treated like the unwanted stepchild. Deliberately guiding and encouraging parents is not an agenda priority.

- New churches are so overwhelmed with getting going that they can't give time to developing children's and youth ministry with any quality.

- Perhaps the biggest category is that of traditional churches who will listen to the concerns, but seem powerless to move away from "the way we've always done it." They're generally quick to point to others as having the problem, and refuse to think seriously that their church may also be infected with ineffectiveness.

Why are all the troubling statistics so rarely connected to what's happening in "my church"?

I think there are three reasons.

THE CRISIS IS UNINTENDED

Everyone *means* well …

Churches mean well. Every church wants to do a good job of raising up their children. No church intends for their teenagers to abandon them once they're out on their own. Children's workers mean the best, and youth workers are passionate about their work with teens.

Parents mean well too. No Christian parent wants his or her child to walk away from God. And I believe nearly all Christian parents *intend* to raise their kids to follow God. But nearly all parents would also admit that good intentions aren't enough. When we think about the issue, we're quick to point a finger of blame toward something else—a wrong peer group, or the anti-Christian education environment, or the overall decadent culture. The fingers point in every direction.

Ministry organizations and suppliers also mean well. Read their ministry vision statements (including that of Awana, my organization)—they're great. We all believe we have *an* answer, if not *the* answer. In the past five years in particular (since Barna's *Champions* book came out), nearly every ministry organization and supplier has addressed the lack of a biblical worldview in kids. We all declare, "Use *us,* and your kids will turn out better." We all desire to *produce* a biblical worldview, and we all believe our ministry and materials help.

But sometimes the help doesn't seem to work.

Recently, Jeremy[9] stopped by to see me. I've known Jeremy since he was a little boy, and he has turned out really great. He's now an associate pastor in a church, and he's thriving in his ministry and in his family. I'm so proud of him! He earned the Citation Award (the top achievement in Awana), and he would tell you his experience as a kid growing up in Awana was a major factor in his spiritual development. Jeremy has a brother who was also a Citation achiever. But his brother walked away from God almost the moment he graduated from high school (outwardly, at least—inwardly it probably happened earlier, or maybe he never truly trusted in Christ at all). As far as I know, the brother has never come back.

We never mean for the young people who go through our programs to turn out like Jeremy's brother, but sometimes they do.

None of us *mean* to have dismal results. So our problem is not that we lack good intentions—we've got that covered.

THE CRISIS IS UNMEASURED

A second reason that people believe the problem must be someone else's, not theirs, is that we don't measure the crisis.

We don't measure it because there's embarrassment for parents when their teenager questions their faith, and there's guilt and regret when he or she abandons it. How many families in your church have a son or daughter who has walked away? Is that hard to answer? It's likely you don't have a ready answer, because we don't talk about it much.

A missionary friend of mine, nearing retirement from the mission field, has three sons. Two have gone on in ministry, one has walked away from God entirely. He talks a lot about the two, but rarely mentions the other son. I understand—it's uncomfortable.

We also don't measure the crisis because they're off to college or moved to another town, so it's now someone else's problem. The "fruit of our church" becomes invisible, because it's gone. Families move. People switch churches. So if a young adult falls away, it doesn't get included in any church growth statistics.

Have you ever heard of a church attempting to find out how the children who grew up in their children's ministry and youth group turned out? It's just too hard for a church to undertake. So we really *don't* know how ours are turning out. The lack of measurement makes it easy to shame the national picture while feeling little concern about our own situation.

Plus, measuring seems so corporate, so inappropriate to ministry. After all, we say, it's impossible to measure what's in a heart, so how can we really know if any measurement is accurate? The rationalizing keeps us from doing it. So when it comes to our church, we just really don't know what the picture is.

THE CRISIS IS UNDERAPPRECIATED

The third reason we're slow to accept the immediacy of the crisis is that we haven't believed the research. Not *really*.

I've had conversations with dozens of children's ministry leaders who have attempted change, but have met resistance. Parents are slow to respond, and church leaders are slow to provide a new emphasis to children's ministry and parental responsibility. It's like no one really believes the crisis is truly a crisis.

Maybe we need a 9/11-like experience to wake us up. On 9/10, our government leaders were their typical bickering, partisan, I'm-right-and-you're-wrong selves, much more willing to point out differences than to recognize commonalities. I know that you know what happened on the morning of 9/11, but do you remember what happened in the evening? A miracle occurred in the rotunda of the Capitol building. Do you remember? Republicans and Democrats put aside their differences, joined hands, and were united in a prayer meeting!

What made such a difference in just twenty-four hours?

On 9/10, the enemy seemed far away; on 9/11, we knew it was close.

On 9/10, the enemy seemed vague; on 9/11, we knew it was real.

Those two issues—seeing the enemy as *close* and as *real*—are critical to awakening people to action. If the enemy is perceived as real but only far away, we're slow to move. And when we see it as neither real nor close, we're not inclined to move at all.

If parents and churches don't see the enemy as real—if they don't really believe the research about the loss of our young people to the world—they'll likely do very little. If they don't believe the enemy's close—it's only a problem at someone else's church, or in that other denomination, or with someone else's children—they probably won't respond either. Until we can get churches and parents to awaken to the crisis and see it as both real and near, we'll face a difficult battle trying to reverse the trends we see in the research.

We also haven't thought through the implications of this crisis. We haven't peered into the future and understood the threat. We haven't looked long enough at the church of Western Europe and learned from it.

What will happen if there are few young people in the future

who are spiritual champions? Will a passion for evangelism decrease
in the coming decade? Will it become completely passé in churches?
If biblical knowledge is on the decline and biblical worldview nearly
as rare as the needle in the haystack, where will our biblical scholars,
our critical thinkers, come from? If our twentysomethings know
biblical facts, but little or nothing in their lives tells us they're living
out biblical truth, where will the lay leadership of tomorrow come
from?

If we're to continue to propagate Christ's church, we must have a
focus on developing the evangelists of the future, the Bible scholars,
the role models, the pastors, the godly fathers and mothers.

WHY IT'S SO HARD

But it isn't easy.

Our task of raising committed followers of Christ is made more
difficult by the constantly changing face of culture. Today's teenagers
have spent their formative years choosing their own media; they've
selected what news is news, what program is programmed, what
entertainment is entertaining them, and what facts are facts. Meanwhile the pace of technological transformation only accelerates,
leading the way in rapid changes in most other aspects of children's
and youth culture.

This perpetually shifting landscape creates an environment that
greatly fuels the perspective that truth is changeable, relativistic, and
customized—mine for me, yours for you. There are few constants in
our young people's lives.

Our task is also difficult because parents and other role models aren't doing so well either. How many parents are consistently

living out a dynamic faith in front of their children? Many who say they want their children to follow God don't practice godliness at home. They want their children to turn out well, but they're too stuck in their unproductive habits to create the kind of impact that's needed.

As Christian parents struggle to guide their teenagers, they hope and pray the youth group will provide an answer. Thankfully, many youth pastors and lay leaders do (and my church's youth pastor is one of them). They have such a positive, life-changing impact in the lives of teenagers. Yet a youth pastor should never be expected by panicky parents to be their child's "savior." Nor should youth pastors think of themselves that way. I know—I was once one of those youth pastors who felt *I* knew teenagers better than the parents did, and *I* was the one in touch with their world. It never occurred to me to try to partner better with parents and listen to them more.

CAN WE DO BETTER?

Four glaring voids remain in our spiritual training of youth and demand our attention:

1. *No revolution.* The focus on parents taking on their biblical responsibility of spiritually training their children has yet to become a revolutionary force in our churches. For the most part, parents are *still* abdicating their role to the church. We must not let the focus die or even stay the same—*we must grow it!*

2. *No target.* Parents, children's ministries, and youth ministries have no clear target for how a child turns out. Longfellow's lines reflect our approach in discipling youth:

I shot an arrow into the air,

It fell to earth, I knew not where.

3. *No teamwork.* Parents and ministry workers are not integrating their efforts. Rather than a finely coordinated team, they're independent of one another, infrequently communicating and rarely collaborating.

4. *No plan.* It's time to have an intentional approach that spreads across all of the formative years of a young person—not merely one or two or three years. Early childhood must link to elementary; children's ministry to youth ministry; and all align to support the home. We must intentionally design our discipleship processes throughout ages two to eighteen.

Can we do better? *Yes!*

Let's start with establishing a clear target. And we can find it in the Old Testament account of Joseph.

DISCUSSION GUIDE

1. In what ways can you identify with the story of Sarah?

2. What overall impression do you have of the research findings mentioned in this chapter?

3. Do you know what's happening with the youth of *your* church after they leave home? Do you think the results the researchers are finding are indicative of young people in your church?

4. Do you believe the "crisis" mentioned in this chapter is real? Why or why not?

5. In regard to the current crisis with our youth, how aware are we of our enemy's reality? How aware are we of our enemy's closeness?

6. What are the prevalent attitudes in your church regarding parents working together with children's workers and youth workers?

CHAPTER 3

JOSEPH AND AN ANTI-JOSEPH

Comparing the Old Testament Joseph with the New Testament Prodigal Son fascinates me. Their similarities and contrasts are noteworthy. It's as if the Prodigal Son is an antitype of Joseph.

LINKING THE TWO STORIES

Notice the similarities. There are so many:

Joseph	The Prodigal
The story is about a father and his sons.	The story is about a father and his sons.
Jacob had twelve sons. (Gen. 35:22)	There was a man who had two sons. (Luke 15:11)
The focus is on a younger son. (Joseph was the eleventh.)	The focus is on the younger son.
Joseph, a young man of seventeen, was tending the flocks with his brothers. (Gen. 37:2)	The younger one said to his father, "Father, give me my share of the estate." (Luke 15:12)

Joseph	The Prodigal
As a young man, the son was taken away to a far country. His brothers … sold him for twenty shekels of silver to the Ishmaelites, who took him to Egypt. (Gen. 37:28)	As a young man, the son went away to a far country. The younger son … set off for a distant country. (Luke 15:13)
He was in an environment that produced sexual temptation. His master's wife took notice of Joseph and said, "Come to bed with me!" … One day he went into the house to attend to his duties.… She caught him by his cloak and said, "Come to bed with me!" (Gen. 39:7–12)	He was in an environment that produced sexual temptation. There [he] squandered his wealth in wild living. (Luke 15:13)
There was a famine in that far country. The seven years of abundance in Egypt came to an end, and the seven years of famine began, just as Joseph had said. (Gen. 41:53–54)	There was a famine in that far country. After he had spent everything, there was a severe famine in that whole country, and he began to be in need. (Luke 15:14)
He worked for a citizen there. Potiphar, an Egyptian who was one of Pharaoh's officials, the captain of the guard, bought him from the Ishmaelites who had taken him there. The LORD was with Joseph and he prospered, and he lived in the house of his Egyptian master. (Gen. 39:1–2)	He worked for a citizen there. So he went and hired himself out to a citizen of that country, who sent him to his fields to feed pigs. (Luke 15:15)
His father thought he lost a son. They took the ornamented robe back to their father and said, "We found this. Examine it to see whether it is your son's robe." He recognized it and said, "It is my son's robe! Some ferocious animal has devoured him. Joseph has surely been torn to pieces." Then Jacob tore his clothes, put on sackcloth and mourned for his son many days. (Gen. 37:32–34)	His father thought he lost a son. The father said … "For this son of mine was dead and is alive again; he was lost and is found." (Luke 15:22–24)

Joseph	The Prodigal
He had a robe given to him by his father (at the beginning of the story). Now Israel loved Joseph more than any of his other sons, because he had been born to him in his old age; and he made a richly ornamented robe for him. (Gen. 37:3)	He had a robe given to him by his father (at the end of the story). The father said to his servants, "Quick! Bring the best robe and put it on him." (Luke 15:22)
His older brothers were jealous. When his brothers saw that their father loved him more than any of them, they hated him and could not speak a kind word to him. (Gen. 37:4)	His older brother was jealous. The older brother … answered his father, "Look! All these years I've been slaving for you and never disobeyed your orders. Yet you never gave me even a young goat so I could celebrate with my friends. But when this son of yours who has squandered your property with prostitutes comes home, you kill the fattened calf for him!" (Luke 15:28–30)
His brothers were not happy to see him again. Joseph said to his brothers, "I am Joseph!" … But his brothers were not able to answer him, because they were terrified at his presence. (Gen. 45:3)	His brother was not happy to see him again. The older brother became angry and refused to go in. (Luke 15:28)
The father and son had a joyful reunion, and their relationship was restored. As soon as Joseph appeared before him, he threw his arms around his father and wept for a long time. Israel said to Joseph, "Now I am ready to die, since I have seen for myself that you are still alive." (Gen. 46:29–30)	The father and son had a joyful reunion, and their relationship was restored. While he was still a long way off, his father saw him and was filled with compassion for him; he ran to his son, threw his arms around him and kissed him. (Luke 15:20)

The similarities are striking. And so are the contrasts. One story is a true narrative spread over fourteen chapters of Scripture, while the other is a parable (likely fictitious) that Jesus gave in only a couple hundred words.

Other contrasts:

Joseph	The Prodigal
He began life in a far country as a slave. When the Midianite merchants came by, his brothers pulled Joseph up out of the cistern and sold him for twenty shekels of silver to the Ishmaelites, who took him to Egypt.... Meanwhile, the Midianites sold Joseph in Egypt to Potiphar. (Gen. 37:28, 36)	He ended up in a far country like a slave. So he went and hired himself out to a citizen of that country. (Luke 15:15)
He started in the foreign land with nothing. Now Joseph had been taken down to Egypt. Potiphar ... bought him from the Ishmaelites who had taken him there. (Gen. 39:1)	He started in the foreign land with wealth. The younger one said to his father, "Father, give me my share of the estate." ... Not long after that, the younger son got together all he had, set off for a distant country and there squandered his wealth. (Luke 15:12–13)
He received evil that he didn't deserve. Joseph's master took him and put him in prison. (Gen. 39:20)	He received good that he didn't earn. The younger one said to his father, "Father, give me my share of the estate." So he divided his property between them. (Luke 15:12)
He gained wealth. The LORD was with Joseph and he prospered.... The LORD gave him success in everything he did.... Potiphar put him in charge of his household, and ... the LORD blessed the household of the Egyptian because of Joseph. (Gen. 39:2–5)	He wasted wealth. The younger son ... squandered his wealth in wild living.... He ... spent everything. (Luke 15:13–14)

Joseph	The Prodigal
He ended in the foreign land with wealth and honor.	He ended in the foreign land with nothing but humiliation.
Pharaoh said to Joseph, "I hereby put you in charge of the whole land of Egypt." Then Pharaoh took his signet ring from his finger and put it on Joseph's finger. He dressed him in robes of fine linen and put a gold chain around his neck. He had him ride in a chariot as his second-in-command, and men shouted before him, "Make way!" (Gen. 41:41–43)	He longed to fill his stomach with the pods that the pigs were eating, but no one gave him anything. When he came to his senses, he said, … "I am starving to death!" (Luke 15:16–17)
He repeatedly refused to commit adultery.	He partied with prostitutes until his money was gone.
Though she spoke to Joseph day after day, he refused to go to bed with her or even be with her. (Gen. 39:10; see 39:6–12)	The younger son … squandered his wealth in wild living. (Luke 15:13)
With honor, he brought his father to him.	In disgrace, he returned to his father.
"Tell my father about all the honor accorded me in Egypt and about everything you have seen. And bring my father down here quickly." (Gen. 45:13)	"I will set out and go back to my father and say to him: Father, I have sinned against heaven and against you. I am no longer worthy to be called your son; make me like one of your hired men." So he got up and went to his father. (Luke 15:18–20)
He received a ring from the king.	He received a ring from his father.
Pharaoh took his signet ring from his finger and put it on Joseph's finger. (Gen. 41:42)	The father said to his servants, "Quick! … Put a ring on his finger." (Luke 15:22)

In summary: Joseph exemplified godly wisdom at its best; the Prodigal exemplified human foolishness at its worst.

IS JOSEPH YOUR MODEL?

Let me ask a silly question: Would you rather have your child (or other children in your church) turn out like (1) the Prodigal, or (2) Joseph?

Here's choice one: My child will leave home before he's ready, will waste all of his money—and mine, too—on wild partying, will sleep with prostitutes, will end up with nothing, and will take care of pigs, till he finally comes to his senses.

Some parents (maybe the Prodigal's father too) would say such a life track was necessary to knock some sense into that young man's head. Some kids, it seems, learn only the hard way. But aren't you thankful Jesus didn't end the story with the Prodigal in the pigpen? That kind of an ending wouldn't have addressed the point Jesus wanted to make. We know the Prodigal came to his senses and went back where he belonged, but we're not told if the change that came over him was permanent. We don't know.

However, no parent, given the choice, would want his child to learn the hard way.

Here's choice two: In the most difficult of circumstances (not brought on by himself), my child will have integrity in his work ethic, will repeatedly say no to the temptation of sin, will have faith in God through years of difficulty, will respond to every situation with wisdom, will become a capable, respected leader, will harbor no animosity to those who harmed him, and will provide for me in my old age.

I'll take that one. Joseph is an incredible picture of how we hope our children will turn out. We might not choose the circumstances he had to go through, but we certainly prefer to see our children respond to any difficulties they encounter in the same way Joseph did.

Of course, the response of the child isn't entirely dependent on the parents and the church. Many children have grown up with the best of parents, in a vital, equipping church, and then thumbed their nose at God and abandoned it all. But that reality doesn't diminish the responsibility of parents and churches to do all they can to raise a Joseph.

Now, a serious question: Are you (or others responsible for children and youth in your church) doing the things that will produce Josephs?

Or where you are, is there ...

no revolution?

no target?

no teamwork?

no plan?

DISCUSSION GUIDE

1. Go back to the first chapter, and review the facts of the Most Difficult Moment as they were described for the father of Joseph and the father of the Prodigal. What similarities and differences were there?

2. What similarities between the stories of Joseph and the Prodigal do you find to be the most significant? Which are less significant? Why?

3. What contrasts between the two stories do you find most fascinating? Why?

4. React to this statement: "Joseph is an incredible picture of how we hope our children will turn out."

5. Do you think the parents in your church are doing the things that will produce Josephs?

6. What does your children's and youth ministry need to produce Josephs?

CHAPTER 4

A CLEAR TARGET

As I write this, I'm sitting on an airplane beside a young father. (I'll call him John.) We've just finished an hour-long conversation. John's career is enabling young Internet start-up companies to be successful. His company was recently purchased by Yahoo, and he's returning from their headquarters.

I asked John, "So what do you like best about your job?"

His eyes brightened, and he told me of the satisfaction he gets in developing strategy and identifying vision for the companies he serves.

John then asked me what I did, and I told him about my work for a children's ministry.

Thinking he was a good candidate to help me with some content for this book, I asked him, "Do you mind if I ask you a question?"

He was ready to cooperate: "Sure."

I asked him, "Do you have children?"

"Yes, two—they're four and one."

"Here's my question: What do you want to be able to say about your children when they're thirty?"

"Wow," he remarked. There was silence for a few moments. "I've never thought that far in the future. College-educated, I guess—and in a good career. Happily married."

He wasn't going where I wanted him to. "Let me ask a different question. What would cause you to grieve if you *have* to say it about your children when they're thirty?"

"Oh … that they're lost." His answer was the first indication to me that he was a Christian dad. After a pause, he kept on: "Or if I had to say they'd failed morally. Or were addicted to something."

I probed further. "Do you know when you have the best opportunity to impact the answer to that question?"

"No, when?" He was now fully engaged.

"Before they're twelve. The major attitudes of life are formed by then. And the basic foundations for decision-making are in place before the teen years."

I could tell I had his attention. I zeroed in: "So your specialty at work is developing strategy for companies, helping them set vision, yet you've never thought of having one for your own children?"

"No." He paused, clearly stunned. "No. Wow, *no!*" He perked up. "Am I glad I sat next to you!" This Christian dad had never given any thought to what would produce the most important long-term results in his children. I could see the wheels begin to turn.

Then I began to tell him about Joseph.

Why Joseph? Because he portrays for us a clear picture—*a target*—for what our kids should be like when we've relinquished  control over them. It's like having the box cover to look at before you put the jigsaw puzzle together.

John is like so many of us. In the most foundational of relationships—parent-child—parents rarely have a defined target. Test it: Just ask parents, "What would you want your child to be at age thirty?" See if they have a ready answer. I predict that many will respond with a career choice, or with some version of "happy." Some might say, "I want my child to be a committed Christian," or "I want my child to follow God." But very few will give you a clearly detailed answer that demonstrates direction and guidance.

Look at what Psalm 78:5–7 says about God's intention for parents:

> He decreed statutes for Jacob
> and established the law in Israel,
> which he commanded our forefathers
> to teach their children,
> so the next generation would know them,
> even the children yet to be born,
> and they in turn would tell their children.
> Then they would put their trust in God
> and would not forget his deeds
> but would keep his commands.

We *must* have a clear vision for our children—even one that's multigenerational—so we'll be intentional every day to pass along to them the things of God. The clearer the vision, the better we'll know what to do on a daily basis. The fuzzier the vision, the harder it is to be faithful to train our children daily in their spiritual development.

MASTER LIFE THREADS

Joseph provides that clear model or target for the parent, and also for the children's worker and youth worker in the church. For such a biblical model, we could also pick Daniel, or David, or Timothy, or Esther, or Ruth—but I'm proposing Joseph. Here's why:

First, *Joseph was seventeen* when he was taken from home (Gen. 37:2). It's fascinating to me that he's the only biblical model we might pick whose age is given in Scripture. Seventeen—so close to the age when kids today leave for college, find a job, or join the military. It's a time of significant life change for most young people today, and it certainly was for Joseph. While we're told nothing of what his parents did to pass on their faith in God to him, it's pretty clear his personal values and worldview were firmly in place by the time he was taken from home.

Second, *there's a lot of narrative about Joseph*. Only the stories of Daniel and David rival Joseph's in length. We have many instructions for Timothy, but know little about his life story, especially during his teenage years. Most of David's stories have to do with his later life. While he's called a man after God's own heart, he was also an adulterer and murderer, hardly the model behavior we would hold up for our young people.

Daniel's story presents a strong and consistently godly model. But I find the Joseph narrative to be more to the point for today's

youth, because *Joseph's situation presents the greatest test of the faith*
that could face a young person: a hedonistic culture opposed to God,
continual temptation, extreme physical and mental hardships, and
zero spiritual support. Joseph was *all alone*. His family would never
have known if he had given in to Potiphar's wife, compromised to
avoid Pharaoh's jail, or padded his own pocket when he was rul-
ing. There was no external support to keep him on the straight and
narrow; it was only his own integrity, his own heart. Slavery, impris-
onment, language barriers, cultural change—the list of challenges
for Joseph's faith was long. Yet in facing it all, he remained faithful,
righteous, and committed to God.

I find Joseph's model to be particularly helpful because it gives
us five specifics—I'm calling them the Master Life Threads—that
enable us to have a clear target for raising our own children.

Why Master Life Threads? Because these specific character qualities
must not be simply inserted as a segment of a scope and sequence, nor
a theme in a curriculum. Rather, they must be woven throughout all of
a child's spiritual training, from birth to that Most Difficult Moment.
They become integral in conversations, in lessons, in relationships.

Let's look at five passages in Genesis that show us these life
threads. Look especially at the *words* of Joseph when he speaks of
God. I believe they're very telling about his character.

MASTER LIFE THREAD 1: RESPECT

We don't know how much time went by before Joseph became
overseer of the house of Potiphar. He may well have had a swift rise.
I think we can safely assume he was still young, maybe even still a
teenager, when he began facing temptation from Potiphar's wife:

Now Joseph was well-built and handsome, and after a while his master's wife took notice of Joseph and said, "Come to bed with me!"

But he refused. "With me in charge," he told her, "my master does not concern himself with anything in the house; everything he owns he has entrusted to my care. No one is greater in this house than I am. My master has withheld nothing from me except you, because you are his wife. How then could I do such a wicked thing and sin against God?" (Gen. 39:6–9)

His words here show us that *Joseph had learned respect.* He took his job seriously.

There's a progression in his response that's worthy of note:

- *He respected authority,* and was determined not to do anything that would erode his master's trust in him. When Mrs. Potiphar tried to get him into bed, he saw that temptation first as a violation of his relationship with Potiphar. His first reason for not giving in to her was the authority he'd been given—he refused to dishonor that.
- *He respected the sanctity of marriage:* "You are his wife." Any hanky-panky with Mrs. Potiphar would violate his value system that regarded the marriage relationship as sacred. You'd think such a statement would cause some hesitation on the part of Mrs. P, but evidently it was no obstruction to her.
- *He respected right and wrong.* "A wicked thing" is how Joseph

refers to a rendezvous with her. I doubt this had much impact on Joseph's seductress either, but it was obviously a huge deterrent to him. He's saying, "This is just *wrong.*" God's standard for purity had been deeply ingrained in him, and he just couldn't see himself violating that standard: "How could I do such a wicked thing?" It was beyond what he could imagine. The particular wording of this phrase gives us great insight into Joseph's heart.

• *He respected God.* He saw a wrong against Potiphar as a sin against God. Somehow, Joseph had learned a correct view of God's holiness, and it served as an absolute barrier between Joseph and this temptation. Those last four words—"and sin against God"—are meaningless unless you have a worldview—a heart—that interprets daily circumstances in light of God's character and plan. This sounds much more personal than just violating a standard; to give in to this woman would injure *his relationship with God.*

Joseph's perspective is simply amazing. Think of it: Here's a young man—maybe still a teenager—who interprets a temptation in the realm of the *flesh* as a sin against *God.* What would it take to develop such a perspective in our teenagers today?

Teach Your Children Respect

1. Teach your children to *respect* human authority.
2. Teach them to *respect* human relationships.
3. Teach them to *respect* God's standards.
4. Teach them to *respect* God.

MASTER LIFE THREAD 2: WISDOM

Joseph was in prison—imprisoned unjustly, because Potiphar's wife lied about him. You could excuse Joseph if he became somewhat bitter about his circumstances—after all, to first be sold by your brothers as a slave, then be thrown into a dungeon because of false accusations, is pretty tough to take.

I've seen an ancient prison on the coast of West Africa—an underground, windowless dungeon hollowed out in the rock. The stories about it from our tour guide left me numb. It was used by slave traders to hold captured Africans until they could be transported by ship to Europe or America. The only opening was from above, where newly captured people and food were thrown through. Though the cell was only about twenty by thirty feet, our guide said it often held a hundred people. There was no room for them to lie down to sleep, no drainage for urine or excrement, no removing the bodies of those who died.

I don't know if Joseph's prison was like that, but it was likely much worse than our prisons today.

Joseph and two of Pharaoh's men were in the prison together. Each of the two men—Pharaoh's cupbearer and his baker—had a dream the same night, and each dream had a meaning of its own.

> When Joseph came to them the next morning, he saw that they were dejected. So he asked Pharaoh's officials who were in custody with him in his master's house, "Why are your faces so sad today?"
>
> "We both had dreams," they answered, "but there is no one to interpret them."

> Then Joseph said to them, "Do not interpretations
> belong to God? Tell me your dreams." (Gen. 40:6–8)

In these words of Joseph, we learn more about him.

First, *he saw God as the source of wisdom.* "Do not interpretations belong to God?" Understanding and interpreting a dream is no easy matter for anyone in any culture. And in Egypt, where there was a whole profession devoted to such things, the baker and the cupbearer could hardly expect Joseph to do it. They must have thought, "How could he possibly have the knowledge, the wisdom, or the interpretive skills necessary? After all, Joseph isn't even an Egyptian, let alone a magician or a wise man."

But Joseph saw things differently. He knew wisdom had nothing to do with a culture, or with a profession, but with a relationship—with God. He knew God was the source of wisdom.

Another thing we learn here about Joseph is that *he was confident in his relationship with the God of wisdom.* By itself, his "Tell me your dreams" statement might indicate Joseph was far too confident in his own wisdom. But he preceded it with "Do not interpretations belong to God?" Out of his relationship with the Almighty, he could speak with bold certainty because of his reliance on God's wisdom. It is also significant that he did not say, "Do not interpretations belong to God? Tell *Him* your dreams." His words are telling: He as much as said, "I know Him."

Such confidence is extraordinary. Think about your young people. Do they leave the nest knowing in their hearts that God is the source of wisdom, and that they can personally rely on that wisdom?

Today, our children certainly *can* be confident in their relation-ship with God. But how do we help them?

First, make sure they have that relationship. And it will be dif-ficult for you to lead them into a relationship with God if you don't have one first! That relationship comes by trusting in Jesus Christ's death on the cross and in His resurrection. That trust brings forgive-ness of sins and eternal life—and entry into God's family. So begin by teaching them the gospel, then give them opportunities to respond by faith when the Holy Spirit draws them to God. Continue to point them to God's ability and God's attributes. Some children's workers and parents instead point their children to an outward action—such as "going forward," praying a prayer, or being baptized—as evidence that they're a child of God. Outward actions are no proof; anyone can fake an outward action or be fooled by one. Our children's con-fidence should be in God the Savior, in who He is and what He has done, and in His ability to save.

Second, weave in-depth knowledge of Scripture into your children's spiritual training. Today, Bible knowledge is being pooh-poohed by some in the Christian educational community and by some in children's ministry as well. Testing of Bible knowledge in a number of Christian universities is being supplanted by "more rel-evant" measures. The assumption is that simply learning Bible facts, Bible trivia, is inadequate—and I couldn't agree more. But let's not throw out the baby with the bathwater; just because Bible knowledge isn't the *end* doesn't mean it's not essential as a foundation. Thor-oughly learning God's Word, including the details of the lives of people He used, is an important foundation for wisdom.

At the same time, some churches are replacing more traditional learning of Bible stories and what they reveal about God with me-centered, character-based studies. Is this trend good? Essentially, no. Developing character is a wonderful thing. But godly character is *not* the foundation; it's the house that's formed on top of the foundation. God's truth is the foundation, and learning and comprehending it should come first.

Remember, it *is* possible for a person to have knowledge without wisdom, but it's pretty hard to have wisdom without knowledge. Following the same logic, it's also possible for a person to have great biblical knowledge but not godly wisdom, yet it's highly unlikely anyone would have godly wisdom without knowledge of biblical truth.

To summarize, learning the stories of the Bible and gaining from them a deep appreciation and reverence for God and His work in the lives of His people is a critical step in a child's development of wisdom.

Teach Your Children Wisdom

1. Teach your children to know that wisdom is based upon God's truth.
2. Build into them the biblical foundations for wisdom.
3. Teach them to have confidence in relying on God's wisdom. This of course means that they come to *know* His wisdom—His Word.

In Genesis 42:18, these first two life characteristics of respect and wisdom are underscored. Joseph sees a group of brothers from Canaan, and knows they're *his* brothers (although they don't recognize him). He begins testing them by putting them in prison. But after three days, he releases them and says to them, "Do this [follow my instructions] and you will live, for I fear [respect and honor] God." Joseph had confidence in what he said, not because of his education or his intelligence, but because of his heart-view of God.

Think about your children today: Once they've put their trust in Jesus Christ as Savior, what single truth is more important for that child to have deeply ingrained in his or her heart than a fear of God?

Do you see the connection? Again and again we're told in Proverbs that fearing (respecting) God is where wisdom begins. "The fear of the LORD is the beginning of wisdom, and knowledge of the Holy One is understanding" (Prov. 9:10). Wisdom is a critical starting point.

Teach your children to respect God's authority. Then they'll accept His truth, and then truth leads to wisdom.

MASTER LIFE THREAD 3: GRACE

Fast-forward: Joseph has become ruler and administrator over the land of Egypt. Second in authority only to Pharaoh, he skillfully stores away grain to prepare the country for seven years of famine.

Before the predicted famine begins, he enters a new personal stage of life: He becomes a father. We're not told much about this, except for what he names his boys. Of course, they'll come to hold a significant place in biblical history, with two of the twelve tribes of Israel named after them.

In our culture, naming a child is a big deal, but in a different way than in biblical times. We want a name that sounds cool, memorializes Grandpa, etc., but we usually don't put much significance in the name's meaning. Maybe it's because we're not entirely sure of the original meaning of names anymore. But in Old Testament days, names meant something. For the father and mother, it meant memorializing a significant life event, or a belief, or a heart feeling. Remember Naomi? She essentially named her sons Puny (Mahlon) and Pining (Kilion). Why? We're not told, but it must have fit them. She later wanted her own name changed from Naomi (meaning "pleasant") to Mara (meaning "bitter"). God changed the name of Abram (meaning "exalted father") to Abraham ("father of a multitude"); Jacob's (meaning "trickster") name was changed to Israel ("he fights with God") after he wrestled with an angel. The meaning of names was significant.

So when Joseph named his two sons, it likely was something he first thought about a lot. Surely their names reflected the most important lessons he'd learned about life:

> Joseph named his firstborn Manasseh and said, "It is because *God has made me forget all my trouble and all my father's household."* The second son he named Ephraim and said, "It is because *God has made me fruitful in the land of my suffering."* (Gen. 41:51–52)

In this case, we're not left guessing about what Joseph meant when he named his sons, or trusting some Hebrew scholar to tell us. It's right in the text. With Manasseh's name, Joseph tells us what he'd given up—bitterness and revenge. With Ephraim's name, we learn what he gained—grace and blessing.

Joseph demonstrated grace. Joseph had learned to give grace, mercy, and forgiveness, and to receive blessing. And notice that this happened *after* he had achieved a position of great authority, and *before* his brothers came to Egypt. He had the power to avenge the wrongs done to him, which makes his response even more remarkable. At this point in his life, Joseph could have punished Potiphar's wife to clear his name, and he could have executed revenge on Potiphar. He might even have sent an Egyptian army unit to find his brothers and teach them a lesson or two. He could have found the cupbearer who forgot him for so long, and had the man thrown back in prison. Yet instead Joseph was gracious; he gave each of these people the forgiveness they didn't deserve.

I know a family that yells at each other all the time. The mom is the biggest yeller, but her kids are nearly as bad—she's done a masterful job of teaching them how. Anytime she's offended, she gets mad and yells. When the kids don't do what she wants, she screams at them. I've heard her on the other end of the phone, shrieking at them over minor issues. Her kids are learning from her that you have to fight to defend your own rights, stay mad and bitter when you're infringed upon, continually bring up past hurts, and hold a grudge until you finally get your way.

I'm really concerned for those children. Their future jobs are in jeopardy. Their future marriages are in jeopardy. They stand little chance of general peace and enjoyment of life unless they can break free from their mother's pattern.

Joseph's example is opposite. He refused to let wrongs done to him affect his heart or his actions. He says, "*God made me forget.*" He knew God was the author of grace and mercy, and he gave Him the credit. But it's interesting that he didn't say, "God made me *forgive.*" Now, his past trouble wasn't erased entirely from his memory; after all, the name he gave his son refers to it. But as far as the hurt and the desire for revenge were concerned, the offense against him was forgotten.

I've learned over the years that I can forgive a wrong, but forgetting it is a whole new level. With some deep hurts, I've had to consciously forgive again and again—even on a daily basis. But I couldn't keep from thinking about those things that hurt.

If you were in Joseph's shoes, how could you forget your brothers selling you as a slave? You couldn't by yourself—but you could by relying on God.

Joseph *forgot*. The offense deserved to be remembered, but God helped him forgive and forget. *That* is grace.

Joseph also *received* grace. He could have taken credit for his rise to power, his patience, his wisdom, his exceptional administrative ability in preparing for the famine. But he didn't; he recognized and proclaimed that all the good happening to him came from God. That goes against human nature: We all like to keep at least a little credit for ourselves, even if we give some to God. But Joseph gave God the praise.

Teach Your Children Grace
1. Teach your children to respond with grace and mercy when wronged.
2. Teach them to view good things they enjoy as coming from the grace of God.

How our children respond *after* pain, *after* discipline, and *after* difficulty must be a major focus of parenting. Their response is a major determining factor in their life happiness. They must be taught to respond with grace. It's a primary life skill.

As a parent, how do you teach this to your children? There will be dozens of opportunities, I'm sure. Let me emphasize the most important one: At an early age, show a deep reverence for the message of the gospel, and share it with them often. When your children come to understand that they've wronged God, that they're sinners, and that God has offered them mercy, it gives them the spiritual basis for doing the same with others.

Of course, our children must *receive* mercy too. They don't deserve the forgiveness that comes when they place their trust in Jesus Christ and His death on the cross as the payment for God's requirement for their sins, yet God provides it. That decision means the Holy Spirit then comes and lives within them, empowering them to be merciful and gracious to others.

MASTER LIFE THREAD 4: DESTINY

Joseph's brothers had come to Egypt to buy grain because the famine that gripped the land of Egypt also affected Canaan. Of course, they had no idea that this Egyptian ruler they were dealing with was their own brother.

In God's sovereignty, He now used their awful deed of selling Joseph to slave traders years earlier to preserve their lives. Joseph had figured this out, but the brothers had no clue.

As the famine worsened and the brothers came to Egypt a second time to buy grain, Joseph revealed to them his identity:

> Then Joseph said to his brothers, "Come close to me."
> When they had done so, he said, "I am your brother
> Joseph, the one you sold into Egypt! And now, *do not*

be distressed and do not be angry with yourselves for sell-
ing me here, because it was to save lives that God sent me
ahead of you. For two years now there has been famine
in the land, and for the next five years there will not be
plowing and reaping. But *God sent me ahead of you to*
preserve for you a remnant on earth and to save your lives
by a great deliverance.

So then, it was not you who sent me here, but God. He
made me father to Pharaoh, lord of his entire household
and ruler of all Egypt. Now hurry back to my father and
say to him, "This is what your son Joseph says: God has
made me lord of all Egypt. Come down to me; don't
delay. You shall live in the region of Goshen and be near
me—you, your children and grandchildren, your flocks
and herds, and all you have." (Gen. 45:4–10)

I'm amazed that when Joseph told his brothers not to be distressed, he immediately added, "Do not be angry *with yourselves.*"
It appears Joseph was way beyond his own anger, an indication that
when he named Manasseh, he really meant what he said. Instead, his
concern was for his brothers.

Pay attention to two things in this passage that are so significant:

First, *Joseph had a sense of destiny.* By now he had a clear picture
of God's calling on his life. He knew his life had *purpose.* There was a
reason for all that had happened to him. He likely didn't see that purpose clearly when he was being forcibly transported to Egypt by the
slave traders, or when he was in Pharaoh's prison. I believe, though,

that even in the darkness of those times, he trusted that God *did* have a purpose—even if he couldn't see at the moment.

Second, *Joseph's destiny was God's to choose.* Joseph would never have chosen the path his life took; he clearly saw that God had mapped out his life journey. *"God sent me"* is repeated here three times, and again in other passages. He knew God was in control.

Tiger Woods is a prime example of a boy who grew up with a sense of destiny. His father instilled within him the expectation of becoming someone special, and this was a prime driving force throughout his youth. His sense of destiny gave him passion to become the best golfer in the world. I deeply admire that, but I also believe that finding destiny in doing God's will is better.

Another little boy who grew up with a sense of destiny was my cousin's son David. He developed a love for wrestling as a toddler and immediately showed extraordinary talent. By age six, he was scary-scary good. During high school, he broke ten state records and earned three state championships, and at one point was ranked number one in the nation in two styles of wrestling. He won the largest high-school-age tournament in the world, and he gave God all the glory.

David received a full scholarship to the University of Nebraska, and there was talk of potential gold medals in NCAA Championships and even at the next Olympics. But before he could wrestle his first match in college, his destiny came crashing down with a shoulder injury that landed him in the hospital. With six hours of major reconstructive surgery, followed by months and months of rehabilitation, his shoulder wouldn't hold up for him to wrestle again. His hopes were dashed, and his sense of destiny disintegrated.

David knew himself as a *wrestler*. When that was gone, he wasn't sure who he was or what God had for his life.

Fortunately, David was taught as a youth that sometimes God's plans aren't what we think they are. It took David a while to rebound and to see his destiny from a bigger perspective. He knew God was in control and would still provide purpose to his life, and he knew God might even use this huge disappointment for His glory. Today he's able to take the lessons learned in those days of extreme disappointment and help other young wrestlers understand that God's plan may not be our plan; rather, all things work together for good for those who believe.

If our child's sense of destiny is centered in himself and dependent on his own efforts and giftedness, then things out of his control can demolish it. But if his sense of destiny is centered in God's calling and dependent on God's sovereignty, then even very difficult things outside his control can strengthen it.

The role of the Christian parent is to give a sense of destiny that's more specific than we find in the world. Secular parenting authorities tell us to help our children find their destiny; but we Christian parents are to raise our children to find their destiny *in the will and calling of God.*

As a little boy, my godly parents built within me this sense of destiny. I felt God was going to do something special in my life. They drilled into me that my life would be best if I was "in God's will." That topic was one I frequently heard, so that even as a young teenager I had an anticipation set in place: "What would God have for me do? What is His will for my life?" I was persuaded it would be something special. My concern was that I might not recognize it.

I wanted to follow God; I wanted to find out His best. And believe me, that sense of destiny kept me out of a lot of trouble as a teen.

I think this is emphasized less today. We work on godly character, but fail to give a sense of destiny, of purpose.

The temperature of current American culture says that it's cool to let your children make up their own minds about their future, their careers, their life partners. That's certainly different from a couple of centuries ago (or even in other cultures today), when sons were expected to follow in their fathers' trade and parents exerted much more control over their children's decisions.

I'm not advocating going back two centuries. I am proposing that parents and churches strongly influence children from an early age to desire to find their destiny—their purpose—in following God's will.

Teach Your Children Destiny in God's Will

1. Transfer a sense of destiny to your children.
2. Make it clear that destiny is found in following the calling and will of God.

MASTER LIFE THREAD 5: PERSPECTIVE

Jacob, his sons, and their families had moved to Egypt. Joseph saw to it that they were given prime real estate in the land of Rameses (Gen. 47:11), and he provided for them throughout the famine. They intended only to wait out the famine, but ended up staying longer.

After seventeen years, Jacob died. To Joseph's brothers, Jacob's death brought a new concern to the surface—how would Joseph treat them, with their father no longer around? Would he now avenge their treachery against him decades ago?

They were concerned:

> When Joseph's brothers saw that their father was dead, they said, "What if Joseph holds a grudge against us and pays us back for all the wrongs we did to him?" So they sent word to Joseph, saying, "Your father left these instructions before he died: 'This is what you are to say to Joseph: I ask you to forgive your brothers the sins and the wrongs they committed in treating you so badly.' Now please forgive the sins of the servants of the God of your father." When their message came to him, Joseph wept.
>
> His brothers then came and threw themselves down before him. "We are your slaves," they said.
>
> But Joseph said to them, "Don't be afraid. Am I in the place of God? You intended to harm me, but God intended it for good to accomplish what is now being done, the saving of many lives. So then, don't be afraid. I will provide for you and your children." And he reassured them and spoke kindly to them. (Gen. 50:15–21)

Had Romans 8:28 been written at the time, Joseph likely would have recited to his brothers: "And we know that in all things God works for the good of those who love him, who have been called according to his purpose."

As he had earlier when he first revealed his identity to them (Gen. 45:5–7), Joseph repeated to his brothers his sense of destiny, then directed attention to God's plan and sovereignty.

Joseph made these points:

- The brothers' intent was to harm him.
- God's righteous plan overruled the brothers' evil plan, and in fact, used their plan to accomplish His.
- Joseph intended to align his future actions with God's plan ("I will provide for you and your children").

Perspective is so critical. My pastor shared a personal illustration about this in a sermon several months ago. It went something like this:

> I'd just pulled out of the church parking lot, onto the street, to go home after a day in the office when this maniac came flying over the hill behind me in his sports car. He was going at least twenty miles per hour over the speed limit, and I could see him zigzagging in and out of cars behind me. Just the sight maddened me. I had the urge to drift slowly into the other lane, just to slow him down. What kind of lunatic would drive like that? My "road rage" barometer was rising.
>
> Then I determined to change my perspective. I wondered *why* he was driving so crazy. Did he just have a fight with his wife, or did he just get news that his daughter had been taken to the hospital? Maybe he just lost his job.

With a new point of view, my anger abated, and I found myself being able to pray for him—even for the crisis he might be facing. I prayed for God's protection on him and for his salvation.

The right perspective can make such a difference—even keep us from road rage!

Teach Your Children Perspective

1. Teach your children to know that God is in control.
2. Teach them to interpret events in light of God's sovereignty. It's one of the most important things we can do, both as parents and ministry workers. Things *will* go wrong for them, things they didn't cause and have no control over. How they respond is what really matters.

Keeping God's sovereignty in view will bring many benefits:

- *It helps keep them from depression.* When you can see negative events through a lens of faith in God's plan for good, your spirits are kept from sinking to the depths.
- *It helps defuse anger.* We see this so clearly from the story of Joseph. Why was he able to forgive his brothers and then provide for them? Because he saw what had happened in light of God's sovereignty.
- *It helps deflate an overactive ego.* The greatest antidote to pride problems is to instill in your child a belief that God is in control, not him or her. That means realizing that positive

fortune, good times, and special talents are from God, not our own doing.

• *It provides strength in difficult times.* It's like when you tell a child, "This shot won't hurt for long, and it will help keep you from getting sick all year." You're molding the child's perspective, giving him strength to stand the temporary pain because there's a larger benefit. That's what a belief in the sovereignty of God does.

IMAGINE THIS

Earlier we did an extensive comparison of Joseph with the Prodigal Son. Going further, look at how these two differ in regard to these five Master Life Threads:

	Joseph	The Prodigal
Respect	He gets a 10!	Didn't respect his father.
Wisdom	Had it.	Lacked it.
Grace	Gave it to others.	Needed it from others.
Destiny	Followed God's choices.	Followed his own choice.
Perspective	"God is in control."	"I want to control."

Once again, here's a summary of Joseph as a model. Take a minute and just imagine that the children and youth you're responsible for turn out like this:

- Joseph *respected* God's authority.
- Joseph was *wise* and knew his wisdom came from God.
- Joseph practiced *grace* in his relationships.
- Joseph had a great sense of *destiny* in doing God's will.
- Joseph's *perspective* of life started with the sovereignty of God.

HOW DOES IT HAPPEN?

The Christian community in America has been doing battle for a number of decades now over what our youth should be like. Some have defined our ideal Christian youth in terms of externals. In my day, it was all about length—hair length for the guys (shorter was better), and hemline length for the girls (shorter was definitely not better). Some believed good Christian girls couldn't wear pants. Going to movies was out, even if it was *Bambi*. In the last fifteen years, the debate has been about baggy pants, midriffs, tattoos, body piercing, and a host of other concerns.

As a result of this kind of focus, I believe that legalistic standards have produced a false spirituality that has brought confusion and division to the body of Christ, and shame to the reputation of God's people.

Some have reacted with an extreme pendulum swing: "Why have any external standards at all? Let everyone do what they want on the outside; what really matters is your heart." This opposite viewpoint also is unbiblical, and nearly as harmful as the first. It's true the heart is what really matters, but it's not *all* that matters.

Joseph is better than both of those extremes. I'm glad we don't know how long his hair was, or whether he wore baggy clothes, or if he had tattoos, or pierced his body in funny places, or anything else about his external appearance. But we do see his heart, and we see that his actions demonstrated godliness as well.

We definitely want to see children turning out like Joseph. The million-dollar question is, *how?*

The narrative of Joseph doesn't tell us. We don't know what kind of parents Jacob and Rachel were. Jacob was probably not the most ideal father—we know he was partial to Joseph and Benjamin, and he'd been a schemer in his earlier years. Was it Rachel's strong mothering that helped Joseph turn out so well? Or was it simply the Spirit of God at work in him? Any answer we give is only a conjecture.

But not knowing how Joseph became such a model of godliness doesn't negate the usefulness of his story in giving us a clear target.

Let me challenge you to weave these five characteristics of Joseph's—these Master Life Threads—into *every* part of a child's spiritual education. You may choose different characteristics, or more, but don't allow them to be merely a study topic or a curriculum theme. Weave them into the *life* of your child. Weave them *throughout* the life of your child.

You'll learn more in the final chapter about what that looks like. But it won't happen easily, or at all, if you don't follow the exhortations in this next chapter.

DISCUSSION GUIDE

1. Before reading this chapter, how would you have answered this question: What do you want to be able to say about your child when he or she is thirty?

2. How would you answer that question now?

3. Why is it helpful to have a biblical personality, such as Joseph, as a target for our children's spiritual development?

4. What are the limitations of Joseph as a target?

5. Does it make sense to you that learning respect for God's authority comes first in a child's spiritual development? Why or why not?

6. Picture "wisdom" as a house. How would you label the various parts of the house? What does the foundation represent, and the framing, and the roof, etc.?

7. React to this statement: "Grace is a primary life skill."

8. Have you found your destiny in doing God's will? Explain your answer.

9. Think through the benefits of perceiving your circumstances and events in your life in light of God's sovereignty. Then think about your children. Are some of the benefits more applicable to one child than they are to another? Explain.

CHAPTER 5

DREAM TEAM, DREAM TEAMWORK

Contrast two teams:

The U.S. hockey team went into the 1980 Olympics as a group of no-names. They were viewed as undersized and underskilled, and on paper were no match for the mighty Russian team. But in what was known as the Greatest Victory of All Time, they dethroned the Russians and went on to win the gold medal.

Contrast that with the U.S. Olympic basketball team in 1988. Here were perhaps the twelve best players in the world on one team—yet the Russians beat them.

What made the difference?

Teamwork. It trumps talent and technique.

AT OAK STREET CHURCH

What does teamwork look like when it comes to discipling children to *know, love,* and *serve* Jesus Christ?

Let's take a look first at what it *doesn't* look like, as we visit Oak Street Church on the first Sunday of September.

In the youth room, youth pastor Rob watches the new seventh-graders trickle in. There's Andrew, the pudgy redheaded pastor's son who the other kids called Carrottop; George, the loud one; and a new kid he didn't know, short and wiry with dyed-black hair. Then Jessica comes in, a good four inches taller than any of the boys. She slouches into the first chair available.

"Well, here's my new mission field," Rob thinks.

Kids keep coming. He tries to count, but they're moving around too much. He wonders, "Will this group be different?" He hadn't expressed it to anyone, but Rob is secretly relieved that the just-graduated high-school seniors are gone (most of them, anyway). He'd been so frustrated with their lack of desire for spiritual things. *But then, I was their youth pastor for only two years. I didn't really get to guide them from scratch.* Rob hadn't been too impressed with what he heard about the guy who preceded him, and he felt he needed to start over discipling the kids in the group.

The thought of getting the current seventh-graders from the start has energized him. "This will be *my* group," he's told himself. "I'm looking forward to discipling these kids."

"Hey, guys," he says to the kids nearest him, "Am I glad to see you here. I'm Pastor Rob." But he notices that Jessica doesn't respond. She stays slumped in her chair, looking forward. "What's with her?" Rob wonders.

Meanwhile, Martha and Mike are in the fifth-grade room, which is decorated just like they want it—after all, they're starting their twelfth year of teaching fifth-graders, and this room had been theirs the whole time. They love teaching fifth-graders: Mike likes the challenge of overcoming and directing the energy of these ten- and eleven-year-olds; Martha is incredibly creative and loves making learning fun for such a challenging age. She's been looking forward to this day, because in her teaching she's blending in some new ideas she picked up at a recent conference.

"Are we gonna do the creation game this year?" These are Chandra's first words upon coming into the room. Chandra's older sister Jessica was in Martha and Mike's class two years earlier. "Jessica told me it was *so* much fun."

Martha inwardly beams, delighted that a student would tell her younger sister about the class. "As a matter of fact," Martha says with a big smile, "we *are* going to do the creation game again. And you're going to love it."

Then Martha remembers. "Ohhhh, yes, Jessica." Just to keep Jessica involved, Martha often had to totally abandon the lesson and play a game instead. In the end, she'd been relieved when Jessica left the class. *Will Chandra be the same?*

In the three-year-olds room, Eleanor is trying to hang on to little Chrissie, who's screaming because her mother just walked out the door. Eleanor looks around the room at the new little faces she and her helpers are charged with this year. While she doesn't mind serving as director for this age group, Eleanor is thinking, *The next ninety minutes aren't going to be the easiest I've ever had in here.*

She smiles as she remembers a decade ago when she first started working with three-year-olds. She had a screamer back then too—a little girl named Jessica. Eleanor chuckles as her memory fills with the picture of Jessica's mom trying to figure out whether to leave, scold her daughter, or cry.

"I wonder," Eleanor asks herself, "what Jessica thinks now about coming to church?"

Then her thoughts go back to the lesson. Jenny, the children's ministry coordinator, didn't make a decision about curriculum until a week ago, and nothing has arrived yet. Eleanor will have to wing it today. "But then," she tells herself, "it'll be okay if we don't have any Bible teaching this week. After all, it's only the first week of the fall."

Meanwhile Jessica's parents, Rachel and Steve, are putting on their best faces as they walk into an adult class. Roy, the class leader, calls out to them, greeting them by name. Then he asks, "How's your weekend been?"

"Great," Steve lied.

Steve and Rachel have decided they won't tell anyone about the tantrum Jessica threw yesterday when they talked with her about going into the youth group or her griping that filled their car on the way to church this morning. Jessica had always been hard to control, but it was only getting worse. Relieved that she finally submitted to their threats and had actually gone into the youth room, they're praying that somehow Jessica will connect with the youth leaders and will want to keep going back.

Steve and Rachel get their coffee and settle into chairs next to two other couples, but their minds aren't on the lesson.

THE NEED TO INTEGRATE

Our children are receiving a spiritual education that lacks integration.

In the fictional but typical Oak Street Church, the parents and ministry workers are all interested in the spiritual education of the young people God has entrusted to them. They all have good intentions. They're acquainted with one another. They're part of the same church. But *not once* have they ever discussed how they might work together to train their children. In the youth room, Rob sees what he does with seventh-graders as "the beginning." With the fifth-graders, Martha loves to create her own stuff. With the three-year-olds, Eleanor relies on whatever is given to her. And concerned parents Rachel and Steve are becoming very dependent on the church to guide their daughter Jessica.

But Rob the youth pastor doesn't see his young teenagers as people with a history. He hasn't thought about connecting his teaching with what they've learned before. Martha is focused more on the teaching process itself (especially using her gift of creativity) than on her students and their learning. Eleanor is entirely dependent upon curriculum and what's handed to her. As a mother, Rachel has run out of ideas about what to do with Jessica. Her husband, Steve, is embarrassed and doesn't confide to anyone about his deep concerns for his daughter.

All involved.

All in the same church.

All acquainted.

All independent from the others.

No common threads of teaching.

No understanding of what the others are doing or have done.

No communication.

No collaboration.

Oak Street Church has three separate worlds of spiritual development for the youth who attend there. These worlds operate as independent entities in the environs of the larger organism of the church.

Is this the best that Oak Street Church can do?

HOW MUCH EFFECTIVENESS?

Dream with me:

Andrew, or Carrottop, shook Rob's world the second week of youth group. Pastor Rob had developed (with a masterful blend of creativity and his newly acquired video skills) what he felt was a captivating on-screen announcement for a new series he was wanting to teach on creation versus evolution. He was expecting a positive response from the kids. But Andrew, to his surprise, reacted differently: "Oh, are we gonna study that again? We did that last year in Sunday school."

Then Jessica spoke up to ask, "You're not going to play the creation game, are you?" It was the first time she'd said anything in the youth group. "We did that when we were little kids in Martha's class."

Rob was stunned. It hadn't occurred to him that he might pick a topic the kids had recently studied. He asked them, "What else have you studied?"

"We've studied the whole Bible," Jessica quickly responded. She was on the attack. "I'm *sick* of studying the Bible. I've heard every story a hundred times. Can't we talk about something else?"

Rob stammered some reply, then went on with the youth meeting. But he knew he needed to come up with something fresh by the next week.

The next day he called Jenny, who was over children's ministry, to learn more about what his new seventh-graders had encountered back in earlier grades in their Sunday school curriculum. "Jenny, what have my seventh-graders been learning over the past few years?" There was silence for a few seconds at the other end of the phone. "I'd have to think. Martha and Mike always create their own stuff in fifth grade, and in the sixth, we just changed curriculum this fall. Can I get back to you?"

Rob later related his concerns to Jared, his senior pastor: "We don't know what our kids are learning. We've been changing children's ministry coordinators, and there's little to no continuity about what curriculum to use. Jenny says some of our teachers just develop their own stuff, and we don't know what they're teaching. I don't even know what the last youth pastor taught. Isn't there some way we can integrate all our teaching?"

Pastor Jared listened to Rob and his concerns. He remembered times when his own son, Andrew, had complained about hearing the same stuff over and over. "Okay, Rob, I've got an idea. Let's get together and start aligning what we do. But we need to involve more than Jenny. I'd like a couple of parents to join us. Let's start by inviting Rachel and Steve. They're really concerned about what their kids are being taught."

"*Jessica's* parents?" Rob wasn't sure Pastor Jared was thinking clearly.

"Yes, Jessica's parents. I believe they'll be pretty motivated to help us think through this."

The next week, with Rachel, Steve, Jenny, and Pastor Rob assembled in his office, Pastor Jared explained Rob's interest in better integrating what young people in their church were learning. He turned to Rachel and Steve: "I wanted you here, because parents need to be involved from the very beginning of this discussion, since they're the ones most responsible for our children's spiritual training." Steve gave an uncomfortable glance toward Rachel. "In these discussions," Pastor Jared continued, "I'd like you to represent the parents in our church."

Then he turned to the children's ministry coordinator. "And Jenny, you're vital to this discussion because of your responsibility for what we do in our church for the first years of spiritual education.

"It's important that all of you participate in this discussion," he emphasized.

After Rob shared his concerns over the lack of coordination in curriculum, Pastor Jared said, "Isn't the issue more than just coordinating curriculum? Let me ask you all a question. What do we want to be able to say about the young people growing up in our church when they're in their twenties or thirties?

"Let's start with you, Steve. What do you want to say about Jessica when she's, say, twenty-seven?"

"You know, I guess I've never thought that far ahead." After a pause he said, "I guess I want her to be happily married, have a good career, and be actively involved in church. And of course, I'd like a grandson." Everyone smiled.

Jenny answered next. "I'm like Steve, I guess. I've never thought much about it." Rachel and Pastor Rob nodded in agreement.

"Okay, then we're done for today. You've probably never had a five-minute meeting before, have you? But we need to think that through before going forward. We'll never be able to adequately coordinate what our children are learning until first we have a clear picture of the target.

"So this is your assignment for next time: Everyone come back with a picture of what you want our young people to be when they're in their late twenties. And I don't want your picture to be about what they *do*, but rather what they *are*."

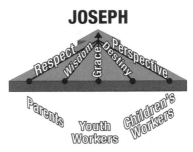

Oak Street Church was on its way. The youth pastor, the children's director, and parents had talked *together*. And they were thinking about defining a clear target.

A TREE ON THE FAR SIDE

Have you ever driven through the heartlands of America and marveled over the straightness of the crop rows as you sail past them on the interstate? How does a farmer get those rows so straight when he plants his fields?

With today's modern technology, tractors come equipped with GPS guidance systems to keep the rows straight. But before that, the farmer would pick out an object on the far side of the field, like a tree, and keep his eyes on it until he reached it. His row would be as straight as his ability to focus squarely on the tree. You could even tell if he looked away by a wiggle in his otherwise straight row.

In plowing the soil for the spiritual life development of a young person, there are way too many wiggles. We're not focused clearly enough or constantly enough on the end result.

In some churches, we haven't correctly identified the tree on the far side. Our vision and purpose statements say nothing about what we want our children to be when parents release their control—when those who were under our care and watchful eye are independent in the world.

Sometimes we have a vision statement for children's and youth ministry, but no one knows what it is. The tree is identified, but no one pays attention to it.

I know of one church that painted its mission statement on the wall of the main hallway in their children's ministry area. But when visiting, I asked several teachers if they could remember what it said. Embarrassed, each one admitted they couldn't remember.

Sometimes a church will have a recognized mission statement for its children's and youth ministry, but it addresses what leaders and teachers do, not how they want the children to turn out. They've identified a tree, but it's the wrong one.

For example, many vision statements read something like this: "We desire to nurture a love for God in our children through a caring, safe environment and through devoted, trained teachers so children grow in their relationship to Christ." Statements like this are more about the activity of the workers or the process of growth in the child than about what we want to see as the finished product.

Here's a better one: "We'll grow our youth to know Jesus Christ, respect God's authority, apply God's wisdom, respond with grace, desire to follow God's destiny for their lives, and perceive all circumstances as under the sovereignty of God."

We're trying to do better at this in my ministry. We've refocused our Awana organization around what we call our Prayer Statement: "That all children and youth will come to know, love, and serve the Lord Jesus Christ." It's simple, but the "know, love, and serve" phrase creates a picture of the young person we desire to produce. It keeps a laserlike focus on the target.

In some churches, there's one vision statement for children's ministry and another for youth ministry, and rarely is there collaboration. It's like a farmer who picks an object halfway across his field and goes to it, then picks out another object on the other side of the field to go the rest of the way. It might line up; then again, it might not.

Sometimes the people in the children's ministry have their act together with their direction and plans, then hand off kids to a youth ministry that wanders all over the place. The youth ministry isn't building on the foundation laid earlier.

Here's a vision statement I found on a church Web site:

> The goal of Children's Ministries is to work alongside parents in helping children establish a strong, Biblical foundation from which to build their lives upon; and develop a faith that, in God's timing, will lead them into a personal relationship with Christ.

That's a good vision statement. It positions parents well, and it focuses on the most important issue, their relationship with Jesus Christ. It's *good,* except it doesn't look far enough into the future. Does it fit with the youth ministry vision? Do parents have a vision?

In other churches, the youth workers are the ones with savvy, and they have their vision clear. But they're very unhappy with what's being produced in the younger-age ministries before they get them. They wonder, "What kind of foundation are the children's workers building in the early years? Do they even have an idea?"

And in some churches, neither the youth nor the children's ministries have a stated vision. They haven't identified any objects at all on the far side of their field.

It's simply crazy to focus only on the process, without a vision for the result. It's like putting a jigsaw puzzle together without ever seeing the picture, building a house without a blueprint, going on a vacation without ever determining your destination—or plowing a field while looking down at your feet the whole time.

Having no clear destination *is* crazy, but we do it in ministry all the time. It's actually fun and challenging as a game, but raising our kids is no game. To approach such a serious endeavor with no vision, no target, is foolishness at best.

And it's not just the church that operates without a clearly defined end result in the critically important task of raising up another godly generation. I'm sure you would agree that the most important task of any Christian home is the raising up of godly offspring, yet parents rarely understand what that means, to say nothing of prioritizing it in their daily lives.

ALL TOGETHER?

Golf is usually an individual sport, but sometimes it's a team competition, as in playing for the Ryder Cup or the Presidents Cup.

For someone like me who really gets into golf, a golf "team" is interesting. Golf teams are made up of individuals who have little or no effect on the performance of the others on their team. The team score is simply the sum of their individual scores. While there's some pairing, it's still pretty much an individual effort.

My other sports passion is football (watching it, not playing). Here things are entirely different. Each player's every move has a huge impact on the success of another teammate's efforts. The linemen must block or the back has no chance to run with the ball. The center must snap the ball perfectly or the quarterback has no chance to even throw a pass. If the punter doesn't do his job well, there's an extra burden on the entire defense. You get the picture.

But imagine a "golf team" approach being applied to a football game. Before a stadium full of spectators, a kicker walks out onto an otherwise empty field. The crowd gets perfectly quiet, obeying all the "Silent!" signs held up at the edge of the field. In this vast calmness, the kicker boots the ball downfield, then walks off as the crowd reacts with polite applause.

An announcer's tranquil voice drifts over the crowd—"And now, ladies and gentlemen ..." He introduces the opposing team's player who'll be returning the ball. All alone on the field, this player picks up the ball and carries it for about twenty yards, prompting another round of pattering applause.

You get the idea. One action at a time—without integration of the efforts of the team members—would turn football into foolishness. It works in golf, but not football.

In the serious "game" of training our children spiritually, our efforts have been more like a golf team, when what we need is a football team approach.

INTEGRATING CHILDREN'S MINISTRY AND YOUTH MINISTRY

It's time for children's ministries and youth ministries to integrate their efforts.

I was a speaker at a weekend children's ministry conference at a large church in a medium-sized city. The youth pastor (who'd been at the church about six months) was an acquaintance of mine, and so he hosted me for dinner the first night. I asked him, "So tell me about the children's director." He paused, thought, then answered, "You know, she's the one staff member I haven't really gotten to know yet."

As the weekend progressed, I could tell that this was one church in which the children's ministry and youth ministry seemed to be living on two different planets. Their philosophies were different, they weren't talking with each other, and the two seemed to be segregated in everything they did.

I attend many conferences for children's workers and some for youth workers. I've noticed that very few ministries are represented at both. It's as if children's ministry and youth ministry are two totally unrelated spheres.

In a majority of churches, there's a wall between the two. It's not a wall of enmity, but one of separation in both philosophy and practice. And it needs to come down.

Remember President Ronald Reagan's historic words in Berlin? "Mr. Gorbachev, tear down this wall!" We need a similar call to leaders in children's and youth ministry: *Tear down this wall!*

TEARING DOWN THE WALL

What does tearing down that wall look like in a local church?

1. *Together, determine a specific target.* I've recommended Joseph as the model. If you have a better one, use it! Talk about what you want your young people to be like in their late twenties or at thirty. Then describe it.

2. *Together, determine Master Life Threads* that will permeate all levels, all programs, and all influencers in the lives of the children of your church. Don't let this morph into an exhaustive scope-and-sequence exercise. This is to provide a clear path to guide materials at all levels.

3. *Together, help parents take their rightful place in the process.* The model you choose will have minimal impact unless these things are present in Christian homes as well as in church.

You may say, "Those action steps are fine, if you're in a position of leadership. But I'm a parent. What can I do?"

A lot! You can start by building awareness in your children's and youth ministry leaders. Talk with them about the need for a clear target. Ask for integration. Start thinking about the long-term picture for your own kids, and encourage other parents to do the same. Don't be afraid to speak up. And whatever you do, do it lovingly and with grace.

PARENTS CAN'T BE FORGOTTEN

Success in this simply won't happen without consistent, committed involvement from parents working hand-in-hand with ministry workers in your church. Why? Because *the home is the most important element*. Without the cooperation of the Christian home, the child is being told Christianity is one thing at church and seeing something entirely different at home. In fact, *the highest-risk young person is not the one from a nonbelieving home, but rather one from a hypocritical Christian home*. A youth from a nonbelieving home doesn't expect home life to be like what the church says—so there's little confusion. Not so with a youth from an uninvolved, unspiritual "Christian" home.

Some will say that we shouldn't be *adding* the involvement of parents; rather, parents should be the *first* involved in spiritually training children. Yes, they should. And if our current overall situation was different, I would express it that way. However, so many parents are *not* involved at all in the spiritual training of their children that by default, children's ministry and youth ministry workers *must* lead. Let's pray that by God's goodness, someday the situation will be different.

So if you're a leader in children's or youth ministry, how do you add the parents into the process?

Here are some ideas:

1. *Be ready for a long journey.* Parents have deeply embedded life habits that may take a long time to change.

2. *Be ready for a major effort.* We're talking about changing the culture, and that won't happen in a day, or with a seminar, or a series of sermons. It must begin with the deep convictions of a

core group of people who are poised to pour major energy into a paradigm shift—preferably the church leadership, including the senior pastor. But don't overlook the power of a group of deeply devoted parents.

3. *Start communicating your vision now, and don't stop.* So often we have the "character quality of the week" or the "theme of the month." Some churches have an annual focus. This is *not* a one-year focus; we must *permanently* change our vision.

4. *Teach scriptural truth* related to the spiritual training of children. After all, God's Word is clear and pointed about the responsibility of parents to train their children in His truth. Let what *He* says become the persuader of parents.

5. *Build momentum through individual relationships.* Remember Jessica's parents, Steve and Rachel? They likely wouldn't have responded to a pulpit announcement or even a first-rate visual "carrot." It took the personal invitation by Pastor Jared to draw them in.

6. *Select those who most feel the need.* That would be parents like Steve and Rachel, or the committed but frustrated Sunday school teacher. Use their frustration to fuel energy and passion.

7. *Continually focus on the target.* If Joseph's life is your target, talk about him often. Plaster your church (as much as you dare) with reminders for the parents to provide focus as well.

8. *Cultivate the core.* If most parents don't respond at first, don't despair. After all, Jesus used the twelve disciples, not the multitudes, to carry out His mission.

Simply setting a clear model and then integrating efforts won't suffice. We need to answer the "how." That demands a clear system of goals, training, reminders, accountability, and recognition. You'll learn about those in the next chapter.

DISCUSSION GUIDE

1. Think about the description of Oak Street Church. How similar is it to a typical Sunday at your church?

2. What is the actual vision and mission of children's ministry and youth ministry in your church? How well is it known?

3. Are those involved in the spiritual development of the youth in your church more like a golf team or a football team?

4. Draw a diagram or express a word picture (like the farmer's field or the golf and football analogy) that illustrates how you perceive your situation. Include in it all who are involved in raising your children spiritually, and how they work together.

5. Where and when will you start taking action? Describe three things you could do, and pick one to do first.

CHAPTER 6

THE JOSEPH PLAN

I love my GPS system. I splurged and got one for the many times I'm driving in a rental car in an unfamiliar city. I hook it up and use it anytime I have even an iota of question about how to get where I'm going. It's just so cool.

All I need is the address of where I'm going, and I'm set. While that female computer voice with the English accent (I chose that one because she sounds so polite) doesn't always take the fastest route as promised, she gets me where I want to go. I just turn left or right whenever she tells me to, and presto—I'm *there*.

And I love the fact that if I miss a turn, she doesn't get upset or flustered; she just gets me back on my route. Even if I decide to make a stop or a detour (flagrantly disobeying her instructions), she never chides me or loses her cool; she just says, "Recalculating … recalculating …" and gets me back on track.

Wouldn't it be wonderful if we had such an automatic guide for raising kids? We could mess up and still get them to grow up the way we want. How cool that would be! We could take detours and make rest stops, and none of that would matter; our kids would still become the godly men and women we desire to produce.

It won't happen, you say?

Well, we can at least dream.

But even if there was a GPS for spiritually training our young people, one person's system wouldn't necessarily work with others.

That's not to say we couldn't use more direction—or become more effective. We *can* do a lot better in fulfilling God's intent for spiritually training our children. And in this chapter, you'll find general guidance to get you started on some specifics.

BETTER THAN GPS

I want to point out that when it comes to raising our kids, there *is* a spiritual parallel to GPS. It's the work of the Holy Spirit in a young person's life. Once our children trust in Jesus Christ as their Savior and Lord, the Spirit lives within them and seeks to guide them as they yield to Him. That's made pretty clear by the apostle Paul:

> Those who live according to the sinful nature have their minds set on what that nature desires; but those who live in accordance with the Spirit have their minds set on what the Spirit desires. The mind of sinful man is death, but the mind controlled by the Spirit is life and peace; the sinful mind is hostile to God. It does not submit to God's law, nor can it do so. Those controlled by the sinful nature cannot please God.

You, however, are controlled not by the sinful nature
but by the Spirit, if the Spirit of God lives in you. And
if anyone does not have the Spirit of Christ, he does not
belong to Christ. (Rom. 8:5–9)

Ultimately, how our kids turn out is between them and God.
The Holy Spirit *will* guide them at each turn if they allow Him to
control their lives. But to simply say, "How my children turn out is
up to God" and not give our own careful thought and attention to
it is to abandon our God-given responsibility, whether we're a parent
or ministry worker or a church volunteer.

It *is* between them and God. No doubt you've often seen how
two siblings raised in a terribly dysfunctional home turn out so differently. One rises above the obstacles (much like Joseph), while the
other succumbs and repeats the dysfunction. You've likely seen the
opposite as well—two siblings raised in a home that's a model of con-
sistency and godliness, yet one of them rejects everything spiritual.
Parents do everything they can, but any child can choose to walk
away from what he or she knows is right, just as the Prodigal did. But
often, just like the Prodigal, they eventually come back to the Lord.

MAKING A PLAN

Remember the people at Oak Street Church? We left them just as
they started working together to make a plan. If I were to advise
them, here's what I'd say:

1. *Your plan must include all involved.* That means children's workers, youth workers, and most importantly, the parents. Maybe not all
are ready to participate, and you need to start with only children's

workers and parents, or only some parents—but start making a plan anyway, as you continue aiming for fuller involvement.

2. *Your plan must be simple.* I've seen "life maps" from several different sources, charting out the spiritual formation of children. Some of them are poster-size or larger, even though written in small type. They were likely created for the professional curriculum developer. But they're far too complex to engage a parent or a volunteer.

Make your plan simple enough that ministry workers and volunteers can remember it when they're busy teaching. You won't be able to align every lesson and every application to the focal points of your plan, but you can weave threads of emphasis throughout whatever you do, so the core concepts are reinforced over the years.

Think of a particular dad in your church who likely reads little. Picture him in your mind. Are you making your plan clear and simple enough that he can and will remember it?

3. *Your plan must have a clear target or model.* Think of an incomplete or blurry blueprint for building a house; it won't do much good. Our target must be clearly defined. (As a clear target for Oak Street Church, I would of course recommend Joseph.)

4. *Your plan must cover all the years of childhood and youth.* I urge you not to segment the plan, and not to think exclusively of your own part in spiritual discipleship (this is especially true for children's and youth leaders). In fact, to honor the exhortation to parents in Psalm 78:5–7, you must also think, "How will we raise *our* children so *they* will raise *their* children to follow God faithfully?"

> He commanded our forefathers
> to teach their children,

so the next generation would know them,
even the children yet to be born,
and they in turn would tell their children.
Then they would put their trust in God
and would not forget his deeds
but would keep his commands. (Ps. 78:5–7)

This also means your plan is not for a year, but for perpetuity. A church that implements a plan like this will be making a "from now on" statement. Parents who make a commitment to a plan are committing to follow it until their children are grown, and even to follow it with their grandchildren.

5. *Your plan must be subdivided into age groups.* I call these groupings "life segments." This allows for age-appropriate emphases, it divides up the task into manageable chunks for both parents and teachers, and it allows for age divisions in church ministry. Yet it's all linked together under the larger picture.

Here's how I think of life segments for children and youth:

Infancy: ages 0–2

Preschool: ages 2–5

Early Elementary: ages 5–8

Elementary: ages 8–11

Middle School: ages 11–14

Senior High: ages 14–18

Two- and three-year periods are good because parents need to be reminded and refocused *regularly.*

Each life segment can have a new focus—a new emphasis on a Master Life Thread. Like this:

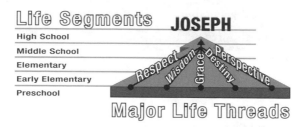

Don't get the idea from this chart that a Master Life Thread is taught *only* in the life segment where it's listed; each is taught throughout a child's growing up. That's why they're called *threads*. But there's an appropriate time to put a special emphasis on each one.

6. *Your plan must be clearly communicated.* This includes both the initial vision as well as the implementation steps. Don't forget the varying personality types that will always be there with your workers and parents. Some will be motivated by the vision's content, others by the excitement and enthusiasm in presenting it. Still others will respond to clear steps that tell them how to do it, while others will need a figurative arm around their shoulder, guiding them through the process.

7. *Your plan must include training.* Dads in particular are reluctant to risk failing, so they're more likely to not even try than to do something they're unsure about. You'll need to decide when and how you'll train parents and workers, but I recommend that it be available once a year at a minimum (and I think the fall season works best).

Require your workers to attend training that will give them the overall picture, then specifics about the age group they're working with. Parents should attend training that will address the age distinctives of their own child or children.

8. *Your plan must include ongoing implementation.* This is not a seminar, or a series; this is a change of culture in your church and in

the homes of your church families. Your church will need to believe this is an important concept to implement permanently.

9. *Your plan must include reinforcement and accountability.* How will you keep parents and workers focused on the same plan for years into the future? We see such rapid movement of families from community to community and church to church, so workers in children's and youth ministry have a challenging task. But regular, encouraging communication, helpful mentors, and an agreed-upon accountability system can be effective.

10. *Your plan must include celebration.* The milestones of spiritual growth in the lives of your children should receive all the attention a birthday brings—maybe even more. It's amazing how parents go all out to celebrate birthdays, when a child doesn't do anything to deserve them except to keep breathing. You'll respond of course that birthday celebrations are about showing love, not recognizing achievement. I agree. But shouldn't Christian parents do a lot more to celebrate a child putting their faith in Christ for salvation, or a decision to obey Christ and be baptized, or a commitment to stay sexually pure until marriage?

A FEW KEY ELEMENTS

Let me suggest a few key elements for your plan that should fit smoothly into what's already happening at most churches.

A PARENT TRAINING SEMINAR

It's not my intent to lay out a whole parent training seminar for you in this book. But parent training is extremely important. Ask your parents, "How many of you have had godly parenting modeled for you sufficiently, so that you know what it is?" You'll quickly learn what a great need there is for training.

Remember, training is more than teaching; for true learning to take place, the process requires demonstration and participation.

Dads in particular need a demonstration. Many aren't likely to risk failure (i.e., trying something they're not confident in) without learning by watching first.

A PARENT COMMITMENT CEREMONY

Baby dedications have, I believe, in most churches, become meaningless ritual. Some pastors, feeling the same way, have deleted it from their church calendar.

I'm proposing the opposite solution: Let's completely revamp parent dedications. Let's enhance it and make it meaningful. Instead of a one-time ritual that eases the conscience of the parent and then is forgotten, let's make them regular and specific, refocusing the parents for each new life segment their child enters.

Envision a ceremony for parents each time their child enters a new age grouping. Here's what could happen each time:

Parents of ...	Dedicate themselves to ...
newborns	establishing a godly home environment for their baby.
2-year-olds	teaching their child to respect God's authority.
5-year-olds	building a foundation of Bible truth.
8-year-olds	building a response of grace and mercy.
11-year-olds	developing a sense of destiny in doing God's will.
14-year-olds	developing the perspective that God is sovereign.

You may choose to have a different emphasis than the ones I've listed for each age group (mine fit into the model of Joseph).

The emphasis in the ceremonies is on parents making a public commitment to follow a plan they've drawn up for the next life segment of their child.

MENTORING

Let's bring back the godfathers!

No, not the movie type, but the historical type. The concept of godparents goes back as far as the second century. They were spiritual mentors for new believers, entrusted with the responsibility of supporting and teaching them in their new faith. From about the ninth century on, godparents were expected to be someone who would assist the natural parents in the spiritual training of a child.

Today, many denominations and churches have abandoned the idea of godparents, possibly because of its close association with infant baptism and christening, which aren't a part of their practice or beliefs. Families still name godparents, but it's usually more of a formality than an intentional act to provide more spiritual instruction for the child.

Many churches don't see a practical way to institute godparenting as a ministry element. After all, young families often relocate, and soon either the young family has moved away or the godparents have. The family-godparents union can fade into ineffectiveness.

But in the life segment approach, I suggest assigning or reassigning mentors at the beginning of *each* segment.

I'm sure you agree that most parents could use the help of another, more mature Christian couple committed to assist them in the spiritual training of their children. To have spiritually mature assistance in raising kids ought to be attractive to any parent. Let's work to provide that assistance in our churches.

Build it into your plan. As children begin a new life segment, assist parents in finding and linking up with spiritual mentors who'll be available for the family and the child.

If you want to guide spiritual mentors on what they should do, start with this list:

- *Commit to regularly praying for the child.* This means asking both the child and the parents for prayer requests on a regular basis. Then pray—and let the child know you're praying.
- *Love the child and the parents.* One of my coworkers said, "When I grew up, I thought godparents were just another source for presents. I didn't know it had any spiritual meaning." You may want to give presents, but it shouldn't be the primary way of showing love. If you're mature enough to be a mentor, you know how to love. Just do it.
- *Keep the parents accountable.* Accountable for what? Spiritual focus, spiritual role modeling, spiritual training. This is one of the best ways to show love. Agree on this accountability aspect at the beginning of the relationship, so it's accepted by the parents.

PARENT ASSESSMENT AND CELEBRATION

Do you believe a child's spiritual development will have a greater impact on his or her future than straight As? How about greater impact than his or her soccer team winning a championship?

But which of those gets the biggest celebration?

Why don't parents and churches celebrate spiritual progress more? I think because it's so difficult to measure. And yes, parents might be pressured to celebrate their children's growth even when it's not satisfactory—to cheat, in other words. A lot can be done to caution parents against that, and besides, I believe celebration with that risk is better than no celebration at all.

That's why a parent assessment should precede the celebration. Then the church confirms the parent's assessment prior to the celebration. The celebration recognizes that the child has had positive and satisfactory spiritual development in his or her life.

Why celebration?

- Celebration provides *motivation for the child.* Imagine the impact on your children when their spiritual growth is recognized, and when they see it recognized in other children. It's a positive way of reinforcing the process and each step of a child's progress.
- Celebration provides *accountability for the parent.* Knowing the church will be honoring parents and children for spiritual development holds their feet to the fire—something that's desperately needed.

CHURCH CALENDAR HIGHLIGHTS

If all this feels too overwhelming to you, maybe this outline will help. Here's how these and other related events could fit into your current church schedule:

In the fall:

- All-church awareness (casting vision)
- Parent commitment ceremony
- Assignment of mentors and development of mentor relationships
- Parent training seminar (set up according to life segments)

Throughout the year:

- Follow-up and progress checks by mentors

In the spring:

- Parent assessment of child's progress
- Church celebration of life progress for each child

Notice that not too much is actually being required here; these events can fit in easily to your current church schedule. In fact, your church may already have meetings and events that the above elements could be incorporated into.

HOW IT ALL WORKS TOGETHER

When a child enters a new life segment, the parents attend the training for that segment, then make a commitment around their new focus. Ministry workers also attend the training for the life segment of the age they're working with.

For example, imagine it's September again at Oak Street Church. Joe and Sarah have a two-year-old. They attend the church's training seminar for the second life segment, along with other parents of two-year-olds and the volunteers who work with that age group in the church. In a ceremony before the church, Joe and Sarah accept the challenge to commit to teach their child to respect God's authority and the other truths so important for that age. (They won't attend another seminar or be part of another dedication ceremony until their child turns five and begins another life segment, although they'll continue meanwhile to establish a new plan each year with the same emphasis on teaching their child respect for God's authority.)

Joe and Sarah become connected with a new mentoring couple for their child, and continue being encouraged by their mentors throughout the year.

The following spring, they participate in an assessment of their parenting. By God's grace and their own dedication and hard work, they're pleased with their child's progress, so they participate also in a public celebration.

Are you getting an idea of what you can do? This book's intent isn't to spell out an exact step-by-step plan—though that may be exactly what you're wired to want right now. I encourage you to build your own plan: Determine the life segments best for your situation and your church. Set your own calendar. Determine your own focus.

In the final chapter, you'll see more information about the sequence of the Master Life Threads, when to emphasize them, and practical ways to weave them into your family and church life.

DISCUSSION GUIDE

1. Why is having a plan so important?

2. How will you respond to parents when they say, "I've done

all I can, and my kids still haven't turned out the way I hoped they would"?

3. Put yourself in the position of a parent of a five-year-old. For that child, how would you implement this plan over the next three years?

4. Discuss the relative value of (a) a time of dedication for parents, (b) accountability, and (c) celebration at milestones.

5. Discuss what you can do from your position (as a parent, children's worker, or youth worker) to begin taking action.

CHAPTER 7

CONNECTING LIFE THREADS WITH LIFE SEGMENTS

Remember again that the principles we drew from Joseph's life are called *threads*—concepts to weave throughout all you do to spiritually develop your young people, whether in the home or in the church.

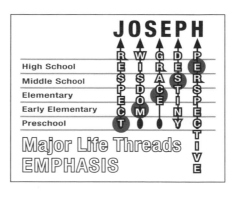

You'll want to teach your children many, many other things, of course, but these five are vital threads, or themes, to weave into the fabric of all your spiritual instruction, whether you're a teacher or a parent.

Let me remind you also how each Master Life Thread can be

appropriately emphasized in a particular life segment: For example, since *fear of God* is the *beginning of wisdom,* it's appropriate to emphasize learning respect for God's authority in the preschool years.

Here's a summary perspective for each Master Life Thread:

Respect

- *When:* Emphasize especially in preschool
- *God-focus:* His authority
- *Heart issue:* How they view authority
- *Bible foundation:* "The fear of the LORD is the beginning of wisdom, and knowledge of the Holy One is understanding." (Prov. 9:10)

Wisdom

- *When:* Emphasize especially in early elementary
- *God-focus:* His truth
- *Heart issue:* How they view truth
- *Bible foundation:* "From infancy you have known the holy Scriptures, which are able to make you wise for salvation through faith in Christ Jesus." (2 Tim. 3:15)

Grace

- *When:* Emphasize especially in elementary
- *God-focus:* His mercy and grace
- *Heart issue:* How they treat others
- *Bible foundation:* "For the grace of God that brings salvation has appeared to all men. It teaches us to say 'No' to

ungodliness and worldly passions, and to live self-controlled, upright and godly lives in this present age." (Titus 2:11–12)

Destiny

- *When:* Emphasize especially in middle school
- *God-focus:* His plan
- *Heart issue:* How they view themselves
- *Bible foundation:* "Offer your bodies as living sacrifices, holy and pleasing to God—this is your spiritual act of worship." (Rom. 12:1)

Perspective

- *When:* Emphasize especially in senior high
- *God-focus:* His sovereignty
- *Heart issue:* How they view the world
- *Bible foundation:* "I am the LORD, and there is no other; apart from me there is no God. I will strengthen you, though you have not acknowledged me, so that from the rising of the sun to the place of its setting men may know there is none besides me. I am the LORD, and there is no other. I form the light and create darkness, I bring prosperity and create disaster; I, the LORD, do all these things." (Isa. 45:5–7)

Let's take a closer look at each of these five Master Life Threads.

RESPECT

What's the first principle a child should learn, spiritually speaking?

God's answer:

The fear of the LORD is the beginning of wisdom, and knowledge of the Holy One is understanding. (Prov. 9:10)

JOSEPH

	R E S P E C T	W I S D O M	G R A C E	D E S T I N Y	P E R S P E C T I V E
High School					
Middle School					
Elementary					
Early Elementary					
Preschool					

Major Life Threads EMPHASIS

I'm sure you understand that "fear" in this verse doesn't refer to the emotion resulting from a sense of danger; it's the "reverential awe" and "worshipful amazement" that results in willing obedience. It's the *highest* form of respect.

Respect for authority is a big deal. There's national frustration with the lack of respect for authority in our schools and in society in general. Teachers complain about it and blame parents. Some parents blame the youth culture, others blame the schools or their own parents. Everyone blames video games but no one does anything about that. Politicians say we have to do something, but all they do is talk. Meanwhile, prisons are full because of the absence of respect.

It *is* a problem. We need to restore respect for authority, and we need to do it now.

It's not a new issue. All of us, from the time we're born, push against the limits placed upon us by authorities. It has been that way since Adam. It's a basic response of the old sinful nature. Every parent struggles to instill respect in every child.

But Christian parents and children's workers have a loftier task than simply instilling in their children respect for authority. We're to teach them to respect *God's* authority. We often don't think how important that is. We want them to respect us, respect others' property, respect teachers, respect the government and laws, and respect church leadership. But the ultimate goal is to respect God's authority. When our children respect Him, others will be respected as well.

When do we teach respect? Throughout all their growing-up years. This starts as soon as they can respond to us. We need to teach infants that no means no, yes means yes. The critical time to focus on this is in the early years of a child's life. Why? Because it's foundational to their learning throughout the rest of life. I'll quote it again: "The fear of the LORD is the beginning of wisdom." That's where we start.

Respect must be earned. Think about this:

- When someone who's *not respected* demands obedience, it results in bitterness, rejection, and ultimately rebellion.
- When someone who's *worthy of respect* demands obedience, it results in acceptance, devotion, and imitation.
- If we don't help our children see God as worthy of respect, we can't expect them to want to obey Him.
- If we're successful in helping our children see God as worthy of our respect, we'll see them want to follow Him.

So what do we do? First, understand that we're the first "Jesus" our children will see. In a way, we represent God to them, so helping them respect us is the starting point. Early in a child's life, parents must begin to teach respect—while we're being respectable at the same time.

Remember that respect is eroded by ...

- our broken promises.
- our unfair rules.
- our partiality.
- our inconsistent discipline.
- our hypocritical example.

Most Christian parents know this. Yet they don't go on to include this next point: Teach the character of God diligently to them. The subject matter of early childhood should develop a deep wonder and awe of God. For example, we should talk about His creation, His power, His holiness (in words they can understand, of course), and His goodness.

"Jesus is my friend" doesn't do it. I believe too much of our Christian literature for young children tries to create warm, fuzzy feelings about God. *Friendliness* with God isn't the beginning of wisdom; *fearing* God is. We must be creating a deep admiration and reverence for God in the preschool years in particular.

WISDOM

What follows next?

God's answer:

From infancy you have known the holy Scriptures, which are

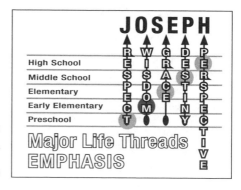

able to make you wise for salvation through faith in
Christ Jesus. (2 Tim. 3:15)

That's the apostle Paul's comment concerning Timothy's spiri-
tual formation. What made him wise? Knowing the Holy Scriptures.
And he learned them from *family*—his mother and grandmother.
Wisdom comes from knowing truth.

Knowledge of God's Word is a big deal. In fact, let me make a bold
statement: *Without knowledge of God's truth, godly wisdom isn't going
to happen.* Your children can have common sense and good judgment
learned from experience, great insight, and knowledge gained from
academic study, but they won't have godly wisdom without knowing
His truth.

Joseph knew that. That's why he told his two fellow prisoners:
"Do not interpretations belong to God?" (Gen. 40:8).

Earlier I mentioned how a number of Christian colleges and
universities are reporting a decline in scriptural knowledge of their
incoming freshmen. I doubt any believer would say that's a good
thing. Yet we keep forging ahead with choices in our homes and
in our churches that contribute to the continued decline. In other
words, we don't think the result is good, but we're not willing to do
much about it ourselves.

Will you be a part of the change? Will you make God's Word a
big deal?

When do we teach wisdom? Like respect, wisdom is taught
throughout life. I don't think of myself yet as being wise; do you?
It's a lifelong journey. But preschool through middle elementary are
prime years to instill in our children a foundation of Bible truth.

They soak up knowledge, so we must make sure they learn major biblical truths about God, Christ, man, the Scriptures, and more.

No one would want to live in a house that was *only* a foundation, but no one would want a house without one either. Remember the parable Jesus told of the wise man and the foolish man, and the houses they built? Jesus said the rock that the wise man built upon was the Word of God. We also are wise life-builders when we make sure our children have a strong truth base.

Why Bible knowledge? To teach our children wisdom, we build a strong foundation of biblical knowledge. We follow the instructions of Scripture:

> These commandments that I give you today are to be upon your hearts. Impress them on your children. Talk about them when you sit at home and when you walk along the road, when you lie down and when you get up. Tie them as symbols on your hands and bind them on your foreheads. Write them on the doorframes of your houses and on your gates. (Deut. 6:6–9)

It's good that our children *learn about* God's Word; it's better when they *learn* God's Word, because that's the foundation for later application to life.

Jennifer Lea Perkins studied differences in biblical worldview scores among adolescents from Southern Baptist families. She focused on 309 students and their parents, representing various levels of family functioning and family discipleship.[10]

In her interviews with both students and their parents, she

found that the parents' worldview was the most important factor in students' worldview. She found four themes that drove a biblical worldview in children:

- frequency and nature of spiritual interaction
- communication within family relationships
- family rituals and routines
- priority and use of family time

(Take a minute to compare those findings with the words in Deuteronomy 6:6–9 quoted above. Do you see any parallels?)

Perkins has a fascinating conclusion regarding Bible reading and family devotions:

> Students in families who do not read the Bible together but only engage in family devotions reported significantly lower worldview scores than other groups—even the group in which no formal discipleship occurs in the home. Only when families engaged routinely in both Bible reading and family devotions were student worldview scores higher than those who do not have routine discipleship activities in the home.[11]

In her "Recommendations for Further Study," she writes:

> In light of the relative ineffectiveness of families who use devotionals without Bible reading in family discipleship activities, research is needed to evaluate different

popular devotional materials for their effectiveness in teaching Biblical truths and values.[12]

So what do we do? Let's teach our children *the Bible*, not just teach them *about* it.

Just as learning respect for God's authority is appropriate as an emphasis in preschool years, so is building a biblical foundation appropriate for early elementary children and beyond. Their little minds are sponges, and we must take advantage of that to build a strong biblical foundation.

Here are some practical suggestions:

1. *READ THE BIBLE!* Sorry for yelling in type, but I don't want you to miss it. Do you know only one of twenty Christian families read the Bible in the home? How much is the Bible read in your children's programs at church, and by you parents at home?

Just do it! Get a plan going, and stick to it.

Many dads struggle with how to lead family devotions. Men, it's not that hard; just *read the Bible.* After time, you will learn to ask questions (and field them) that will add great meaning to your time with the family.

What do you read? Start by reading the major passages that tell the story of redemption from Adam to Jesus. (Don't spend a lot of time in Leviticus or Ezekiel, for example.) And focus on two things in your Bible reading: *fear* (awesome reverence) *of God* and *Jesus' person and work.* Focus on Jesus even when you read Old Testament stories.

2. *Play Bible games together.* Not all of them are focused on Bible trivia; some do a better job than others at bringing out biblical truths and values.

3. *Examine curriculum.* For your children's and youth ministries at church, as well as what you find at home, look for books, videos, and other tools of learning that have high Scripture content.

4. *Memorize Scripture.* It's a wonderful discipline to equip your children for life. Remember that the goal is retention and understanding of God's truth for life, not just mere recitation.

5. *Focus on major biblical truths,* not just the interesting stories. They must learn that God is the Creator, Jesus is the only way, heaven and hell are real, man is a sinner, and sin must be paid for.

What about salvation? Did you notice how Paul in 2 Timothy 3:15 said the Holy Scriptures are "able to make you wise *for salvation* through faith in Christ Jesus"?

The most important salvation truths you must communicate are those about Jesus' death on the cross as the payment for our sins, and what your child must do to have eternal life. *Parents:* Don't leave that to Sunday school teachers or youth workers! *Teachers and youth workers:* Don't leave that to parents! Make sure you're *all* communicating God's plan of salvation to children.

GRACE

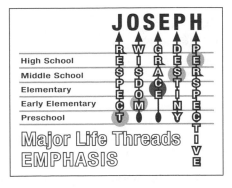

Take any household with siblings and you're bound to hear these three words at least once a day: "That's not fair!"

When Mom responds, "Well, *life* isn't fair, so deal with it!" she's essentially saying, "Learn to respond with grace."

Why grace?

Grace characterized the life of Jesus:

> The Word became flesh and made his dwelling among us. We have seen his glory, the glory of the One and Only, who came from the Father, full of grace and truth. (John 1:14)

Full of *grace*. That's what characterized all of Jesus' interactions with others. If we desire to be like Jesus, we'll exhibit grace as our primary response to unfairness, insults, and difficulties.

We exercise grace when we give others what isn't deserved: the best view of the TV; the biggest helping of dessert; help in homework.

Grace is a big deal. Why? Because grace is a primary life skill.

Few of us are tested when everything's going well, but how we react toward others when things go wrong for us is the indicator of who we really are. Will we exercise grace?

As believers in Jesus Christ, grace and mercy are what we receive *from* God even though we've sinned against Him; they're also what we give to others *because we know Him.* To not extend grace and mercy to others is to be selfish, vengeful, and bitter—qualities that destroy a good life.

But there's another reason: It's the way of salvation. We're saved *by grace*, and so are our children. If they haven't understood this earlier, we must prioritize it as a focus during the middle elementary years. Why? Because that's when children are most receptive to the gospel. All the research I've seen indicates that a majority of believers trusted Christ during their childhood years, *and the others wish they had.* It's a window of opportunity that we dare not overlook. Parents and children's workers must focus on presenting the gospel regularly and clearly during the early and middle childhood years.

Do you believe in eternity? If your answer's yes, then you believe that leading your child to faith in Christ is the most important responsibility you have. See that your children know the gospel clearly, so they'll respond by faith when the Holy Spirit draws them. That's the most critical responsibility of any parent or church worker.

See the little dot below, and the line next to it?

. _____

The dot is less than 1/64 of an inch (0.040 cm) in diameter. Let it represent the typical life span on earth. Let the line represent eternity (though of course, to be a better representation, the line would have no end). If we spend our efforts as parents and teachers preparing them for merely the last half of the "dot," and totally ignored the long line, we're very shortsighted. But that's exactly what we do in our everyday schedules. We think more about preparing them for life than for eternity.

I've become acquainted with Bill and Elizabeth Mitchell, the parents of five children. Last year they lost their thirteen-year-old son James to a massive rejection of a transplanted heart. Their story is incredibly moving—from the moment, only hours after his birth, when they found out James had serious heart problems, through the ordeal as well as the miracle of a heart transplant when he was four, and the subsequent years of both joy and trepidation as they loved him but knew that any moment God could take him home. When they talk about James, they describe a young boy with a huge anticipation of eternity. They talk about his amazing love for Scripture—he was reading through the Bible for the third time when he died. They relate his desire to work with younger kids and to help them to know God.

For the Mitchells, their son's passing was a deep time of grief, as it would be for any parent. But it was also a time of peace. Elizabeth now speaks regularly, sharing their story to encourage other parents. She says, "I had peace, because I knew James was prepared for heaven." And she makes this point: "Parents usually see their role as preparing their children for life, but really, their role is to prepare their children for death." Do you understand what she's saying? Where your children will spend eternity is the most critical issue facing both you and them.

They need to understand God's grace, appreciate God's grace, and receive God's grace by faith. That's the most important decision of life because it affects eternity. So don't focus on the dot and neglect the line.

That's not to say we shouldn't spend any time preparing them for this life. We should. But grace is also a key ingredient in that as well. *Receiving God's grace* is essential to *giving* grace to others. Think about the challenges your kids will face as they grow:

- How to handle an unreasonable boss. (It will take grace.)
- How to respond appropriately when cut off on a freeway. (It will take grace.)
- How to be a testimony when cut from the basketball team. (It will take grace.)
- How to respond when their own teenager gets into trouble. (It will take grace and mercy.)

When do we teach grace? "Throughout life" is the answer again (you've probably figured that out by now). But as with the other Master Life Threads, there's a particular time to emphasize this one.

There are two reasons why the middle elementary years are critical for teaching grace. First, as I mentioned earlier, those are the prime years for children to respond to the gospel, so we prioritize teaching about salvation. If our children get past this window of time without trusting in Jesus Christ as Savior, then the chances that they'll respond at all continue to diminish.

Do we *wait* until these years to share the gospel? Of course not—younger children can understand the gospel, and some will respond earlier. But the middle elementary years is when we really emphasize it.

Second, those are the years when children really begin to independently socialize outside the family. Grace, along with mercy and love, are ways that we reflect Jesus Christ through our social interactions.

So what do we do? We teach children diligently about God's grace and encourage them to demonstrate it to others:

1. *Make sure you're clear about the gospel.* What is the gospel? The apostle Paul said: "I want to remind you of the gospel I preached to you ... that Christ died for our sins according to the Scriptures, that he was buried, that he was raised on the third day according to the Scriptures" (1 Cor. 15:1–4). The heart of the gospel message is the death of God's Son on the cross in payment for my sins, and His subsequent resurrection. Make sure your children know that message—and that Christ did it *for them personally.* Then make sure they understand that being good, going to church, performing

rituals, or having Christian parents doesn't save them. The Bible is clear that we're saved by faith in Jesus Christ. Tell them they need to trust in Jesus Christ and His death on the cross for their eternal salvation.

2. *Make sure they're not trusting in an action.* In many churches, salvation "invitations" have long been a tradition. I believe they can be effective, but they can also be misleading to a child. If a child thinks the outward action of going forward or praying out loud makes him a Christian, he'll be confused. Make sure it's clear that a decision of his heart—his will—is the key.

3. *Create an awe of God's grace.* Encourage them to read stories of people's conversion experiences. Tell them about people you know who have experienced God's grace. Explain to them (this is especially critical for children being raised in Christian homes) that if they hadn't had the privilege of learning early about God, they too might have a bad past. Teach them to be grateful for God's grace in their lives.

4. *Constantly reinforce grace as a life skill.* Tell them, "You might be the only Jesus someone else will ever see," and train them to be aware of the testimony they're living before others. Help them to respond to unfairness, hurts, and insults just like Jesus did—with grace.

DESTINY

What do I want my child to be when he or she grows up?

God's answer:

I urge you, brothers, in view of God's mercy,

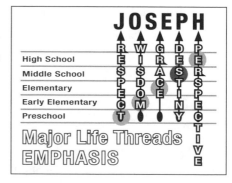

to offer your bodies as living sacrifices, holy and pleasing to God—this is your spiritual act of worship. (Rom. 12:1)

Early adolescence is the time when the drive for significance and acceptance by others begins kicking into high gear.

Think about what provides significance:

Destiny is a big deal. Many philosophers have posited that life's most important question is, Why am I here? Christian parents and children's and youth workers have the responsibility to help young people see that the answer is found in fulfilling God's purpose for their lives.

Here's what a sense of God's purpose for their lives will do:

- A sense of destiny *gives direction* in the major decisions of life. The young person who believes God is calling him or her to serve Him will consider that when deciding what college to attend, who to marry, and what to do for a career.
- A sense of destiny *gives meaning* to life's opportunities. If I believe God might use me to influence children as an elementary school teacher, I'll seek opportunities that contribute to that direction.
- A sense of destiny *provides strength* in hard times. If I understand that God may need to knock off some rough corners in order to best use me, difficult times can be understood and endured.

Your children must feel that they're important to God, that He has a great plan for their lives, and that by submitting sacrificially to Him, their lives will please Him. Teach them that being a doctor or lawyer, or even president, is not the pinnacle of achievement, but rather to be right in the center of God's plan for their lives.

When do we teach destiny? From the time children can understand it, of course. But preadolescence and early adolescence is the time to emphasize it. Middle-schoolers are just beginning to think about what they'll do with their lives.

That was true for me. I was thirteen when a speaker at a summer camp challenged us to commit our lives to following God's will. I can still feel the sense of peace, exhilaration, and significance that came over me when I told my counselor later that night that I felt God was calling me to serve Him with my whole life. Of course, I didn't know then what this would mean, but that decision affected many future decisions—including staying out of a lot of sin—during my high-school years and beyond.

So what do we do?

1. *Teach children they're important to God.* Help them be able to say:

- My life is important because God made me just the way I am.
- My life is important because God loves me enough to die for me.
- My life is important because God has a purpose for me.

2. *Teach them to desire God's will.*

- Read to them, or have them read, missionary stories or biographies of faithful Christians. Get videos about the lives of spiritual giants and watch them together as a family.

- Provide as much exposure as you can to Christian workers, pastors, missionaries, and others. My daughter and son-in-law, Andrea and Ray, recently took their children (my grandkids) to a Christian concert and stayed afterward to talk to the musicians about their ministry. The kids were starstruck, talking for days afterward about it, and now they want to be Christian musicians. I know God will likely lead them differently in life, but that experience will make serving God with their lives more desirable to them.

- Change your vocabulary. Don't say, "What do you want to be?" and expect a vocational answer. Say, "What does *God* want you to be?"—and expect a ministry answer.

3. *Give them service opportunities early.* Many churches and parents wait far too long to get children involved in serving God. Don't wait until the midteen years and then send them on a mission trip where they paint fences and take clothing to the poor. When they're ten or eleven, let them assist in spiritual responsibilities both at home and at church—leading worship, planning, teaching, reading Scripture, planning activities, and yes, mission trips.

PERSPECTIVE

How should my child view the world?

God's answer:

I am the LORD, and there is no other;

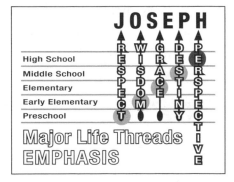

apart from me there is no God.

I will strengthen you,

though you have not acknowledged me,

so that from the rising of the sun

to the place of its setting

men may know there is none besides me.

I am the LORD, and there is no other.

I form the light and create darkness,

I bring prosperity and create disaster;

I, the LORD, do all these things. (Isa. 45:5–7)

God *is* in control. Do your children believe it in their hearts?

Perspective is a big deal. If they believe God's in control, they're ready to face success and failure, health and illness—whatever life throws at them.

While teaching children this throughout life is vital, the teenage years often bring much deeper questions concerning God's control: Why is there suffering in the world? Why does God allow war? If God is in control, then why did my friend get killed in a car accident? Why do I have to take my driver's test again?

Their viewpoint of life and of the world will craft all of their decision-making in the future. It's their *worldview.* They'll filter all facts and interpret all information through it, and all their relationships will be influenced by it.

You won't be able to keep the children God gave you from difficult trials and temptations. They'll face the death of a loved one, financial collapse, and deep disappointment and hurts caused by others. They'll fail themselves, doing stupid things and yielding to sin. No matter how we would like it to be different, they won't be free from those things (neither will we) until heaven. We can't keep them from hurt and pain.

But we *can* mold and influence how they respond. Will they get angry and bitter? Will they fall into depression? Will they seek revenge? Will they repeat the negative behavior?

Knowing that our good and loving God sees the big picture and is in control will provide hope and a positive outlook on whatever comes our kids' way.

The teenage years are the time for spiritual mentors to provide answers to all those difficult questions—honest, biblical answers. While certainly molding a child's perspective is a task for every life segment, we must really hone in on it during the high-school years.

When do we teach perspective? Everything we've discussed throughout this chapter will build perspective in our children. During the senior-high years, we *cement* the perspective that God is sovereign in place. Younger children mimic the perspective of their parents or spiritual mentors, but by the midteen years, they're thinking for themselves. Their faith—or lack of it—is becoming their own. Making faith their own is a natural and important process that we must wisely guide while we encourage critical thinking.

If we don't face the difficult questions and concepts with them before they leave the nest, they'll surely be confronted on their own afterward. Which is better? Do you want your young adult struggling by himself with whether God was in control of creation or whether it happened by chance? Or do you want him to think about it when you're with him?

So what do we do?

1. *Wrestle through questions of God's sovereignty* together with your teenager. Yes, there may be many questions you don't know the answer to, but study and learn together.

2. *Have conversations about personal crises and disappointments.* Help your teenager see things from God's point of view. I use the story of Mahlon and Kilion, husbands of Ruth and Orpah, who died too early, yet God used their deaths to push Ruth to accompany Naomi back to Israel. There she met Boaz, and their marriage resulted in the birth of Obed, whom God used to continue the messianic lineage. Mahlon and Kilion *never knew* what God would accomplish through their sickness, but He was certainly in control.

When positive things happen to your teenager, talk about Esther. She could have gloated about being chosen for her beauty, but instead saw her selection as part of God's plan to do something more important.

3. *Give them a plaque* for their room—in their style of decor—that says, "God is in control."

4. *Keep communication open.* This is vital—they won't come to you again if you act horrified at their questions or comments. This is so fundamental, but I've seen youth pastors completely shut down ministry to kids by rebuking them for their questions. I've had kids tell me their parents yelled at them because they expressed doubt about their faith. That kind of a response *kills* further discussion. I'm sure you know that—just don't forget it when *your* teenager risks a question.

5. *Love them unconditionally,* even when their perspective is wrong or their behavior is sinful. No matter what they do, reflect Jesus to them. Remember, when *He* forgives, He also forgets. Parents can

destroy relationships with their teens by harboring hurts, reminding of offenses, and holding on to bitterness.

MY PRAYER FOR YOU

Are you motivated to get started with the adventure of effectively discipling children?

Set a clear target.

Make a plan.

Work together.

And start a revolution—in your church and in your home.

> *Lord, enable the reader of this book to prioritize the spiritual training of the children and youths You've given them. May he or she have a clear focus for guiding young lives, strong partnerships with others who are also involved, and a good understanding of what can be done step-by-step.*
>
> *Father, may You return the hearts of parents—especially dads—to their children. May You cause each local church and their various ministries to work as one.*
>
> *May You, Father, make this reader a living example of Christlikeness to the youth he or she mentors.*
>
> *In the name of Christ my Savior,*
>
> *Amen.*

DISCUSSION GUIDE

1. In young children, why is it so important to focus first on building respect for God and reverential awe of God?

2. Which Master Life Thread are you doing the best at? What have you been doing in this area?

3. Which Master Life Thread have you been neglecting? How can you begin doing better?

4. Which is the most important thread for the children and youth you're responsible for?

5. What's the most significant thing you've learned from this book?

NOTES

1. Not her real name.

2. The Barna Group, "Most Twentysomethings Put Christianity on the Shelf Following Spiritually Active Teen Years," Sept. 11, 2006, www.barna.org/FlexPage. aspx?Page=BarnaUpdate&BarnaUpdateID=245 (accessed July 14, 2008).

3. Josh McDowell, *The Last Christian Generation* (Holiday, FL: Green Key, 2006), 13.

4. LifeWay, "LifeWay Research Uncovers Reasons 18 to 22 Year Olds Drop Out of Church," www.lifeway.com/lwc/article_main_page/0,1703,A%253D1659 49%2526M%253D200906,00.html (accessed July 14, 2008).

5. The Barna Group, "Teens Evaluate the Church-Based Ministry They Received As Children," July 8, 2003, www.barna.org/FlexPage.aspx?Page=BarnaUpdate &BarnaUpdateID=143 (accessed July 14, 2008).

6. Christian Smith and Melinda Lundquist Denton, *Soul Searching* (New York: Oxford University, 2005), 262.

7. Gary M. Burge, "The Greatest Story Never Read: Recovering biblical literacy in the church," *Christianity Today,* August 9, 1999.

8. Jeremy E. Uecker, Mark D. Regnerus, and Margaret L. Vaaler, "Losing My Religion: The Social Sources of Religious Decline in Early Adulthood," *Social Forces* 85, no. 4 (June 2007): 10.

9. Not his real name.

10. Jennifer Lea Perkins, "Differences in Biblical Worldview Scores of Southern Baptist Adolescents Across Variables of Family Functioning and Family Discipleship" (doctoral dissertation, Southwest Baptist Theological Seminary, September 2007).

11. Ibid., 130.

12. Ibid., 143.

HomeBase is a new program offered by Awana to foster parent-church partnerships and connect families to your church's Awana ministry. Get an overview of how HomeBase works in your church and your home by visiting www.awana.org/homebase.

Visit www.awana.org/store for details on all the products listed in this guide.

⊡⊡ HomeBase®

Parent Resource Guide

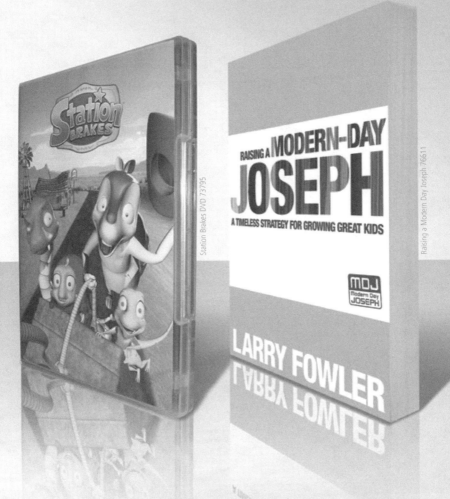

A parent's first and most important business is to spiritually nurture their children. The church's responsibility is to support parents in their spiritual duties. Together you can raise kids to know, love and serve Christ. HomeBase® games and resources give everyone the ability to make homes into discipleship centers for kids.